CW00417318

Making our Connections

Making our Connections

The Spirituality of Travel

Pink Dandelion

Cattorie Adams.

scm press

© Pink Dandelion 2013

Published in 2013 by SCM Press
Editorial office
3rd Floor, Invicta House,
108–114 Golden Lane,
London EC1Y OTG

SCM Press is an imprint of Hymns Ancient & Modern Ltd
(a registered charity)
13A Hellesdon Park Road
Norwich NR6 5DR, UK

www.scmpress.co.uk

All rights reserved. No part of this publication may be reproduced,
stored in a retrieval system, or transmitted,
in any form or by any means, electronic, mechanical,
photocopying or otherwise, without the prior permission of
the publisher, SCM Press.

The Author has asserted his right under the Copyright, Designs and
Patents Act, 1988,
to be identified as the Author of this Work

Scripture quotations are from the New Revised Standard Version
of the Bible, Anglicized Edition, copyright 1989 by the Division of
Christian Education of the National Council of the Churches of
Christ in the USA. Used by permission. All rights reserved.

British Library Cataloguing in Publication data

A catalogue record for this book is available
from the British Library

978 0 334 04408 6

Typeset by Manila Typesetting
Printed and bound by
ScandBook AB, Sweden

Contents

For all Fellow Travellers

Acknowledgements

One of the joys of writing about something we all do, such as travel, is that everyone I spoke to about this book had something wise and wonderful to offer me. I have been very grateful for the insight, interest and support shown me in all these conversations. I also feel a debt to all those who have written about their experience of travel over the years: reading your work has felt like a companionable dialogue, an affirmation of my own aspirations and experiences, that has now lasted decades.

Colleagues at Woodbrooke Quaker Study Centre in Birmingham have been very helpful with offering me space and support to do the writing, and Ian Jackson and Bettina Gray in the library there have helped so much in getting me the texts I needed to consult.

I am grateful to Natalie Watson and her colleagues at SCM for supporting and publishing the work. I thank those who read earlier drafts, and above all my family, who gave me the gift of time and space to make the journey of drafting the text.

'Ben' Pink Dandelion
Clitheroe, February 2013

Preface

Travel and Spirituality

In this book, I am interested in all forms of travel, whether the walk to the supermarket or the round-the-world omnibus expedition, whether a 19-hour day on a bicycle to cover 200 miles or a 19-hour flight from London to Perth. In this way, I define 'travel' in its broadest sense. It is about making a journey, moving from one place to another. I am not just interested in travel made for explicitly religious purposes such as pilgrimage, or travel which turns out to include moments of transforming enlightenment. I also do not make a distinction between travelling and tourism, between what might be seen as 'movement towards' or 'onwards' or 'away from' (the everyday). All are within my use of the term 'travel'.

I have found spirituality a very difficult term to define, and that most people, academics included, use it without even trying to do so. Many say what it entails but not what it is. Often, spirituality is seen as oppositional or differentiated from religion. For example, Paul Heelas and Linda Woodhead in their study of religious decline and the growth of spirituality in Kendal, draw a clear distinction between religion and spirituality (2005). They define religion in terms of a transcendent reference point, such as 'God', and spirituality through a subjective reference point, 'self' (2005, pp. 5–6). This dichotomy provides a useful tool for sociologists interested in secularization and sacralization, but does not work for how I wish to present this discussion of spirituality and travel.

More helpful is my friend Alex Wildwood's maxim that when we are living authentically, we feel 'a part' of the whole, not 'apart' from it. Spirituality for me is about this experience of connection. It is about the awe and wonder we feel when we see the beauty of creation and the connection between every part of it. We see we are not alone in the world, that none of us are strangers in any ultimate sense. This in turn leads us to nurture that sense of the collective whole or community. Spirituality de-differentiates humanity in contrast to the hierarchies and separations of modernity. It is about loving our neighbour freely and unconditionally, whoever our neighbour is.

I write as a British Quaker, a member of the Religious Society of Friends. Quakerism was founded in the seventeenth century on the experience of direct encounter with the Divine. George Fox, early Quaker leader, believed this experience was available to everybody and that we are all of equal spiritual worth. Everyone is part of the priesthood, everyone is a minister. Thus, Quakers have no leaders and no 'front' to their 'Meetings'. Early Friends adopted silence and stillness as the way to nurture that sense of encounter into which anyone might offer 'vocal ministry' as led to by the Spirit. British Friends continue this tradition today.

The experience of the Divine was a transforming one and those converted to the movement adopted a new and distinct lifestyle. They refused to accept worldly etiquette around hierarchy, using 'thee' and 'thou' to everyone rather than the deferential 'you'. They refused to use titles or remove their hat, except in prayer. They refused to fight in 'outward wars', as killing contradicted the idea of the spiritual equality of all. They practised this sense of spiritual connection in a very material way. This didn't mean everyone was free to do what they wanted but that killing would not affirm the covenant between the Divine and humanity. Indeed, Quakers were very critical of others, particularly those who claimed that people still needed to listen to sermons or share in the Eucharist, practices which Quakers now saw as anachronistic. However, Quakers were keen to emphasize that everyone was part of God's people and that God was interested in the good of everybody, not just a partial elect. Thus, one of my presuppositions about the nature of authentic spirituality is that it upholds the integrity of all humanity and affirms the spiritual equality of all. It is a spirituality that seeks peace and justice. It is optimistic about human nature and human potential and it is not about correct belief but authentic experience. It is about having regard and care for everybody.

In secular terms, we can understand this kind of attitude as 'cosmopolitanism'. Philosopher Kwame Anthony Appiah summarizes the concept:

> [T]here are two strands that intertwine in the notion of cosmopolitanism. One is the idea that we have obligations to others, obligations that stretch beyond those to whom we are related by the ties of kith and kin or even the more formal ties of shared citizenship. The other is that we take seriously the value not just of a human life but of particular human lives, which means taking an interest in the practices and beliefs that lend them significance. People are different, the cosmopolitan knows, and there is much to learn from our differences . . . Whatever their obligations are to others (or theirs to us) they often have the right to go their own way. (Appiah 2007, p. xiii)

People are different and necessarily and usefully so, but our obligations to others in one way both transcend these differences and are also enriched by engagement with these differences. Cosmopolitans hold two ideals – universal concern and respect for legitimate difference – in tension. These concerns override what Virginia Woolf, niece of Quaker Caroline

Stephen, called 'unreal loyalties' – those, for example, of nation, sex, school, neighbourhood (1938, p. 79). Similarly Leo Tolstoy, inspiration to Gandhi, inveighed against patriotism in 1896 – 'to destroy war, destroy patriotism' (1994, p. 132). We are brought up to see the world in terms of particular concerns rather than universal ones. We are schooled in being proud of our family, our neighbourhood, our nation, but this is often at the expense of universal concern for what is important to those beyond our locality. Indeed, cosmopolitanism is not a common or popular philosophy: notable anti-cosmopolitans such as Hitler and Stalin required a kind of loyalty to one portion of humanity – nation, a class – that ruled out loyalty to all of humanity. Appiah states: 'the one thought cosmopolitans share is that no local loyalty can ever justify forgetting that each human being has responsibilities to every other' (2007, p. xiv).

This is not easy: 'there are times when these two ideals – universal concern and respect for legitimate difference – clash. There's a sense in which cosmopolitanism is the name not of the solution but of the challenge' (2007, p. xiii). Given this, however, Appiah continues: 'Cosmopolitanism is an adventure and an ideal . . . a world in which communities are neatly hived off from one another seems no longer a serious option, if it ever was . . . segregation and seclusion has always been anomalous in our perpetually voyaging species' (p. xviii).

Cosmopolitanism calls on us not to portion off any part of humanity, not to engender any form of 'them and us' as our nations have done repeatedly for so long and continue to do. This is not to claim a relativism of values, that 'anything goes'; some values are local but some values are universal and should be more strongly adhered to. Appiah claims the aspiration is to allow free people the best chance to make their own lives. We will not reach consensus on how to get there or what it may look like, hence the need, above all, for 'conversation': Appiah uses 'conversation' not only for literal talk but also as a metaphor for engagement with the experience and the ideas of others' (2007, p. 85). 'Conversations across boundaries can be delightful, or just vexing: what they mainly are, though, is inevitable' (p. xix). Consensus or agreement is not important. Engagement and living alongside each other with care for each other is.

Authentic spirituality is surely essentially and simply cosmopolitan. We find it in all the great books of spiritual wisdom. The British Quaker book of discipline is full of cosmopolitan theology. One good example:

> Do you respect that of God in everyone though it may be expressed in unfamiliar ways or be difficult to discern? Each of us has a particular experience of God and each must find the way to be true to it. When words are strange or disturbing to you, try to sense where they come from and what has nourished the lives of others. Listen patiently and seek the truth which other people's opinions may contain for you. Avoid hurtful criticism and provocative language. Do not allow the strength of your convictions to betray you into making statements or allegations that are unfair or untrue. Think it possible that you may be mistaken. (Advice 17, *Quaker Faith and Practice* 1995)

The next section begins: 'How can we make the meeting a community in which each person is accepted and nurtured, and strangers are welcome?' (Advice 18, *Quaker Faith and Practice* 1995).

When our spirituality is being nourished, we live within a cosmopolitan attitude. Nobody is a stranger, everyone is a neighbour. We feel connection, not difference. We feel 'located', not dislocated. We know we are in the right place and in the right space. We are alive with love, awe and wonder and we know that everyone is essentially the same and part of the whole. These, then, I suggest, are the criteria for travel that nurtures spirituality.

In turn, this kind of spirituality nurtures a travel born of curiosity and the wish to engage. It nurtures a desire to 'meet' and understand each other, not just to watch or observe. It nurtures a desire to see the whole world. I don't present travel, then, as an environmental evil (although we need to be very mindful of its impact), but as an obvious strategy for our desire to engage. The challenge, I suggest, is how we balance our spiritual motivations with the ease and delights of travel; the proliferation of the possibility (of mobility) often fed by consumerism and framed within an anxiety about time (feeling we must do what we can in the time we have). This book charts some of this challenge and offers a response.

Introduction

I sometimes feel I have been born to travel, that it is part of my vocation or spiritual calling. Since the age of 14, I have been 'going away' and 'heading off'. This was initially by bicycle but as income allowed, I have travelled by motorcycle, car, aeroplane and ship. I have been fortunate enough to have travelled all around the world to see places, to see people or for work. I have had some of my most important spiritual insights and religious experiences 'on the road'. My first sense of 'God' was aboard a Greyhound Bus in the middle of the night outside St Louis, and so many 'holy moments' – when I have felt that amazing combination of awe, wonder and a love that connects all of humanity – have been while walking through foreign cities. All has felt right in the world; I have felt at one with all and everyone around me. My sense of the authentic has been nurtured by motion. In short, the outward physical journey has frequently fed the inward spiritual one.

In this, I am not unusual. The Hebrew and Christian Scriptures, for example, are full of people led by God to travel or those who meet God on the road. Prophets have rarely sat still in one place and often part of their call has been to travel. Pilgrimage has formalized holy travel, and we find millions travelling each year to enhance their faith through visiting particular sites. At my Quaker Meeting, we regularly host groups of those travelling to Pendle Hill to retrace the footsteps of early Quaker leader George Fox, who had a vision of 'a great people to be gathered' at its peak in May 1652. Fox then travelled on to Sedbergh and later Ulverston, and the Quaker movement began as an organized force that summer. There is a strong tradition of travelling for God or finding God as we travel. When Thomas Cook began his excursions in July 1841, aided by the new railway technology, he too saw these organized outings as a way of observing the Divine: 'Surely there can be nothing inimical to religion in going abroad to behold the handiwork of the Great Supreme?' (Swinglehurst 1983, p. 26). Cook took people out of their home environments and allowed them the pleasure of travel and the pleasure of the destination. He produced detailed handbooks so that they would get the most from their journey, and personally accompanied the groups to make sure all the arrangements went smoothly and to answer questions from the curious. He took them 'elsewhere' to see the glory of God's creation and to expand their knowledge of the world. It was head and heart education.

We still hold on to that romantic ideal and much travel is still sold to us in terms of being away from daily routines and pressures, to see places we have always wanted to visit, to come face to face with the exotic, to relax, to reflect, to learn. We travel to broaden the mind, to literally 'expand our horizons'. Or we may just travel to get to work. Or both. But, increasingly, we have become the authors of our own leadings, the agents of our own travel. We typically no longer discern when or when not to 'go'.

The relatively new technologies of travel, railway, ship, car and aeroplane, have revolutionized our ability to travel elsewhere and back again. We can get to the other side of the world with less than 24 hours of flying. In the time trains took to get me from Clitheroe to Plymouth, I flew from Manchester to Tel Aviv. It even cost me the same. In the last 60 years, we have all become mobile, a nation of travellers. Planes have replaced trains as the dominant form of long-distance travel and overseas holidays are commonplace. They are often cheaper than ones based in Britain and usually warmer. I was once told there were two kinds of people, those who travelled and those who had spare rooms to put them up in. Nowadays the non-traveller is rare. In 2010, there were four million air passengers a day (Urry 2011, p. 1). The world has become defined by movement.

Few of us are now able to walk to work. We rely on car, overground and underground trains mainly. In Britain, the 2011 census reported 27 million cars in use or 1.2 per household, an increase of four million since 2001. Cheaper cars and increased levels of disposable income have meant that the chances of being auto-mobile have increased dramatically. New roads, ostensibly built to ease congestion, have allowed us to commute faster and therefore further. In the USA, according to sociologist John Urry, people travel an average of 30 miles a day instead of the 50 yards they would have done in 1800 (2011, pp. 1–2). The Hay Report in January 2012 reported that some people in Britain spend 20 per cent of their income on getting to work. The Trades Union Congress report of 2012 showed that average daily commuting times varied throughout Britain between 44 minutes in Wales to 77 minutes in London and that averages were on the rise (Trades Union Congress 2012). Our working days get longer.

This increase of holiday and work travel has a huge ecological cost. Urry claims that a third of all CO_2 emissions are caused by transport (2011, p. 3). Our desire to travel erodes green space with the building of new airports or roads or railway lines as well as contributing to global warming. I know many who now refuse to fly. We buy cars partly on their fuel efficiency (or reduced running costs), and the makers of popular cars are keen to offer us models that meet the lowest rates of road tax. Boeing tell us their new 787 is 20 per cent more fuel-efficient.

What I am interested in here, however, is what this propensity to travel does to our experience of travel. In turn, how does that experience feed or diminish our spiritual life? Increasingly travel does not live up to the romantic ideal commodified by Thomas Cook. If we travel by train, we become adept at negotiating 'engineering works' or trying to travel at off-peak times. Going by car, radio 'Travel Updates' and GPS technology allows us to plan our routes with the minimum of delay as roads have become so congested. One small accident can cause huge delays; such is the volume of traffic we create. Travelling by plane involves checking ourselves and our bags in, negotiating passport control and security screening before we are freed to fly. Again we may use new technology to check in over the internet, have a boarding pass ready on our smart phone, but the processes, however ameliorated, are still arduous. Planes are cancelled, delayed by weather or grounded by mechanical problems. What might be an idyllic journey may become an ordeal through overcrowding or delay.

Travelling can be no fun at all. Indeed, the journey can become the part of our daily work routine or holiday that we endure, that we need to get through in order to begin whatever it is we have set out to do. Any holy purpose can easily be forgotten or diminished.

Travel is the flagship of modernity. As well as producing goods and transporting them to the market, a market has been made of the transportation of the masses to wherever the employer now chooses to locate, and wherever we are told would be an ideal place to escape the daily grind. As modernity emphasizes differentiation, rationalization and specialization, so the business of travel has followed. It is its own huge market with so many niches. Buying travel, including the means to travel such as a car, is for many of us our biggest annual expenditure, after housing (Urry 2011, p. 116). Now the majority of us are online, we can literally see where we want to go, plan our itineraries and even book our own tickets. The rule of expertise of the travel agents has been democratized, a reformation in the way the travel industry works. We can buy foreign currency even in our Post Offices now. We need to try to get the best deals, make the best plans, make the journey as bearable as possible given its potential to overwhelm us with discomfort and stress. We typically smother the input of the travel experience with additional inputs: books, music and films are regularly used to exclude what is right next to us, to 'help the time pass'. 'Awe and wonder, and the sense of love that connects all humanity' is in danger of being missed altogether. Waking early on an overnight train from Paris to Madrid to see the sun rise over the mountainous backdrop was breath-taking and inspiring: it simply involved looking out of the window, a manoeuvre missed by those plugged into virtual elsewheres. Our overcrowded modes of travel and our mental attempts to circumvent the dis-ease of moving from A to B often foreclose the spiritual elements of the journey. If the journey becomes the ordeal to complete as quickly as possible, we are not open to the myriad ways that the journey itself can feed our spiritual life. We are suffering from a 'travel sickness' of two kinds. First, it comprises a compulsion to regularly leave our home communities and to disassociate from our neighbours and daily routines. Second, it creates the idea that travel is best seen in terms of hardship and ordeal, an idea I admit that can be regularly affirmed by the experience of present-day travelling.

To overcome this condition, I suggest our standard tactic is to try and separate ourselves. We try to separate ourselves from everyone else. We may choose ways of getting to work that are less busy or alter our hours of work. We may choose holiday destinations that are new, 'off the beaten track', or less popular. Money can always buy at least partial isolation: in the first-class compartments of trains, in business and first class on aeroplanes, in exclusive resorts and hotels. We buy comfort but we also buy segregation and privacy. We can travel to an exotic (that is, foreign and rare) location and never see anything of the country it is a part of. We claim we have a lovely holiday and have been indeed 'away from it all'. Chains of standardized luxury western-style hotels mean we are taken from one home environment to another. We rebuild home abroad. The reliability of supply of the same comforts being routinely available has been key to the success of selling travel to so many with such ease. It lay behind Thomas Cook's escorted journeys. Now the experience of being 'there' may be so similar to the experience of being 'here' that we no longer need escorting at all. All we need is to be transferred. In segregated resorts or hotels, we are never really 'there', rather we could be anywhere. We may maintain an identity as a certain kind of traveller or from a certain culture but we do not nurture community in such settings. At the same time, our mobile phones, digital cameras and Facebook updates displaying our travel exploits, even as we experience them, lead me to think that while we are 'away' ever more easily, we are increasingly never really away at all. I am concerned about how this segregation and how being tethered by technology limits the potential travel can offer our spiritual life. With whom do we really engage as we travel? Does our moving from one place to another afford the opportunities to know each other in the things that are eternal, to feel the reality that all humanity is connected beyond race, culture and creed?

I suggest two potential ways to increase the spiritual potential of travel. The first is that we might travel in less segregated ways. We might choose to talk to our travelling companions rather than seeking ways to smother the discomforts of the journey with personal stereos or in-flight films. We could choose to engage with those on the same journey as us. Crisis often breaks through reserve. I can think of a recent medical emergency on a train, or a train being stopped while police managed some drunken football fans or a fire on a plane in Savannah early one morning. These were times I spoke to my neighbours and they spoke to me. We could deliberately choose more communal modes of travel, the local bus rather than the airport shuttle. We could stay in homes rather than hotels. We could travel more slowly, by ship instead of plane for example: four days sleeping on deck with 200 others sailing between Abu Dhabi and Karachi drew out some great conversations and insights. We could cycle or walk.

The second way to increase the spiritual potential is that we might travel less or not at all. Why do we go somewhere else? Do we need to? Might the work meeting happen now by computer or telephone? Do we need to go so far to have a similar experience of holiday? Can we not find similar enchantment in our neighbourhood? Tobias Jones travelled the world visiting communities and returned to Bristol and found much of what he'd been searching for within a square mile of his home (2007). A friend of mine from Essex travelled to India only to find her home was to be in Lancashire. Satish Kumar talks of needing to balance our ecological concerns about flying with the notion of 'love miles', the times we fly to meet family or see friends, or to do good (2008). I am not suggesting we all stop travelling but that we discern our call to travel all the more regularly. Is this really part of what we are called to do? Does it conflict with other spiritual leadings or complement them? Does this travel plan allow us to use our gifts, to fulfil our ministry? We might adopt the Amish spiritual test of such impulses: 'Does this build community?' Without denying all that travel can offer our spiritual lives, we can better decide when and how to travel.

Certainly, the current ways in which we are so unthinkingly mobile need to change. We are harming the planet, harming our relationships with each other by needing to increasingly disassociate, and internalizing a secular approach to humanity and travel. At the same time, the potential to travel and to learn, both in head and heart ways, from these travels has never been greater. I suggest we can reclaim and rediscover an attitude to travel that builds community, and through that enhances our sense of Spirit at work in our lives and in the world.

I

From Call to Commodity

I grew up immersed in the idea of travel. I planned the routes and mapped out the journeys for our annual holidays reached by car. I knew all the abbreviations of the stickers marking the countries other vehicles came from, and foreign number plates on other cars and trucks made me feel excited, part of an international mobile community. As I started to plan my own travels by bicycle, my knowledge of the atlas and then of more detailed maps became intimate. I have planned so many journeys I have never made but also been lucky to plan many I have. I also began to be interested in the means of motion, the machines of carriage – bicycles, motorcycles and cars. The fact that these made travel possible gave them an exalted status. In turn, as travelling seemed a foregone conclusion, why not also aspire to vehicles of style and quality? I longed, and have continued to do so, after all kinds of wheeled vehicles. Essentially, I am a product of the late modernity we find ourselves in. I have been able to travel widely and in a variety of ways. I consume tales of, and temptations to, travel. Travel is romantic. It is exciting and mysterious. It conjures up something I want to be a part of. As such, travel has become a commodity.

Travel as a romanticized or commodified option available to all is a relatively recent phenomenon. Even in the seventeenth century, most people did not travel more than 30 miles from their home. Before then, travel may have been driven by economic imperative as people moved to secure better living conditions or freedom from oppression. People travelled to go to war or for pilgrimage. People travelled because God told them to. In the seventeenth and eighteenth centuries, as war and peace allowed, the elite travelled on 'The Grand Tour' around the European continent to complete their education. Tourism developed in the nineteenth century (Buzard 1993, p. 1), a system of mass transit often following pre-packaged itineraries. Exploration to unknown quarters of the globe continued throughout the nineteenth century, but holidays and commuting have become predominant in today's mobile society. Essentially, travel has become easier and more affordable (in time as well as money), and we have, as a society, taken up the option to go elsewhere.

I draw out two interweaving themes in this chapter, initially using case studies of two Quakers, George Fox and John Woolman. The first theme is the difference between a life dominated by travel (where travel is the mode of living) and where travel is additional to a more stable existence. I suggest that where the journey becomes the interruption to life at home, rather than 'home being the journey', it is prone to becoming merely something we buy, a commodity. When travel is added on to work, either as commute or holiday, it is an additional purchase rather than constituting a mode of life. The second theme is the difference between travel that is motivated by our spiritual life if not compelled by it, and travel where our own desire is the motivation and we act as its agents. When we become the agents of our travel, we have lost our sense of divine indwelling and impelling: the journey loses its sense of the sacred and becomes secular. In other words, our travel becomes a secular fulfilment. It may give us glimpses of the sacred or the spiritual, but its main motivation is simply that we want to go. The Grand Tour and the popular travel that eclipsed it was based on desire, not instruction from God. Romantic notions of 'time away' that we desire or feel we need symbolize both the commodification and secularization of travel. When I looked at all those maps as a teenager, I was not thinking of any spiritual odyssey; rather it was about where I could get to, given my budget and the limitations of the school holidays. I was essentially plotting to 'buy' travel in the same way others might save up for loudspeakers. Wolfgang Schivelbusch wrote that '[f]or the twentieth-century tourist, the world . . . [became] one large department store of countryside and cities' (1986, p. 197). This continues to be true.

Travel as Faithfulness

Travel has always featured in religious discourse. The Christian gospel teaching that a prophet is not honoured in their own land (Mark 6.4, for example) almost entails a divine instruction to travel. God, it seems, has regularly told people where to go. Eve and Adam were the first biblical travellers, Cain was condemned to be a 'wanderer on the earth' (Gen. 4.13, NRSV), then Noah and his family were taken across the flood waters in their Ark. Jacob was nomadic, Joseph was taken to Egypt, and later Moses escaped from Egypt to be told to go back and deliver God's people to 'a land flowing with milk and honey' (Exod. 3.8). Joshua completed this mission. Rarely is a reason given; the instruction is its own authority. In the New Testament, Mary and Joseph needed to travel to Bethlehem for the census and then fled to Egypt with their new baby, Jesus, to escape Herod's envy. Jesus travelled widely, finally to Jerusalem on a donkey. Paul met the risen Christ on the road to Damascus. The apostles travelled extensively. It is travel that is largely 'led' or instructed by God.

As a Quaker, I am part of a tradition that takes God's direct and daily guidance to be key in our understanding of what we are to do. George Fox's foundational insight was

3

that God invited everyone to a direct relationship of transformation and witness. Everyone was equal before God and everyone was a minister. God took the faithful into a new place of intimacy where all the habits and traditions of the Christian Church became anachronistic. There was thus no longer a need for a separated priesthood, separated buildings, a Christian calendar and outward sacraments. The challenge was to listen and act faithfully, to live out one's ministry. As a movement, Quakers have claimed they know what is 'of God' through spiritual experience rather than through Scripture. What has been crucial for Quakers, then, has been the practice of working out what is truly from God, a process we term 'discernment'. Thus, from a Quaker perspective, the biblical travel listed above is travel discerned as a response to God's guidance or call. I come back to this theme in Chapter 5.

Early Quakers were highly itinerant. George Robinson felt 'called' by God to go to Jerusalem in 1662, not as a pilgrim, but as a witness to the forthcoming 'Day of His gathering' (Evans and Cheevers 1663, p. 292) and as a sign of obedience. His journey was arduous and included imprisonment at one point. Once he had 'declared' what he felt he had been led to, he found 'great peace with the Lord' (ibid.). The place was irrelevant to Robinson; what was important was being faithful to his calling. A recent book by Hilary Hinds on the life of George Fox, early Quaker leader, pays special attention to his nomadic ministry (2011, Chapter 5). Fox travelled throughout Britain, to western mainland Europe and to North America and his *Journal* (Smith 1998) reads like a travelogue. He was what I call a 'pure traveller' in that travelling was his mode of life rather than additional to some other activity. He travelled rather than stayed in one stable place, because he felt instructed by God to travel. Both Fox and fellow Quakers like George Robinson talk of being commanded by God to leave home. Thus travel was part of a general obedience to call. Travelling was faithfulness.

For Fox, Hinds argues, walking was his default activity. He enacted his public ministry by walking but also his journal records walking for other purposes (Hinds 2011, p. 104). He walked to reflect. He walked if he could not sleep. He walked to 'wait upon God'. Walking was often a prelude to revelation and Hinds gives the following example:

> And one day, when I had been walking solitarily abroad, and was come home, I was taken up in the love of God, so that I could not but admire the greatness of his love: and while I was in that condition, it was opened unto me by the eternal Light and power, and I therein clearly saw, 'that all was done, and to be done in and by Christ . . .' (Smith 1998, p. 16)

The detail of the journey was not important for Fox and others; it was the process of call, obedience and enactment that was crucial. Fox was not walking to 'find' but walking to 'give'. It was a walking born of certainty. Michel de Certeau casts mystics as those who cannot but walk, such is their perpetual longing:

> He or she is mystic who cannot stop walking and, with the certainty of what is lacking, knows of every place and object that it is not that; one cannot stay there nor be content with that. Desire creates an excess. Places are exceeded, passed, lost behind it. It makes one go further, elsewhere. It lives nowhere. (de Certeau 1992, p. 299)

Fox's accounts and those of other early Friends counter this understanding of the nomadic mystic, although he did at first travel to find answers. Aged 19 in 1643, Fox left his family and his apprenticeship as a leather-worker to pursue his religious quest. He spent a year with a Baptist uncle in London and travelled between the camps of the Parliamentary army where, in this Civil War period, the most radical of religious ideas were circulating. He was already clear that the idea that ministers needed to be trained at Oxbridge universities was false, and decided to spend more time with separatists. However, he did not find ready answers to his religious questions, and it appears he reached a state of depression and despair. He later wrote that his 'hopes in all men were gone' and that he 'had nothing outwardly to help me' (*Quaker Faith and Practice* 1995: 19.02).

> Then I heard a voice which said, 'There is one, even Christ Jesus, that can speak to your condition.' When I heard it, my heart leaped for joy. Then the Lord let me see why there was none upon the earth that could speak to my condition, namely, that I might give Him all the glory; for all are concluded under sin, and shut up in unbelief as I had been, that Jesus Christ might have the pre-eminence who enlightens, and gives grace, and faith, and power. Thus when God doth work, who shall let [hinder] it? And this I knew experimentally [through experience]. (Ibid.)

In this moment, in 1647, Fox experienced direct relationship with God. Critically, this new experience was ongoing and constant. Fox was full of certainty and confidence: from this moment, his *Journal* accounts are full of the transformation he has already experienced (Smith 1998). In a manner different from de Certeau's claim, Fox's walking was not based on longing but on God's instruction to bring everyone to this new covenant with God. He travelled in response to God and as way of life.

Such itinerant preaching was not unusual in this time but Hinds suggests that no other religious group so based its identity on itinerancy (2011, p. 107). In turn, stories of travel formed an important part the self-presentation of the faithful to their peers. Pragmatically, it allowed the network to establish itself and grow further as the leading Friends regularly

visited established and new groups of Quakers. It was walking which identified Quakers as mobile but walking also identified them as those failing to, or refusing to, integrate into
more stable society. Their home was no one place but was
located in an intimacy with God. Miles Halhead's wife said
she wished she had married a drunkard rather than a Quaker
as at least she would know where to find him (*Quaker Faith
and Practice* 1995: 19.10). The early Quakers transcended
convention. They were continually arriving but also leaving.
Hilary Hinds quotes Eric Leed from his book *The Mind of the
Traveller*, 'The departure not only "excorporates" a member
from a social body, it also "incorporates" and inaugurates
the mobile body' (Leed 1991, p. 26). In other words, Quakers
placed themselves outside of the stable communities they visited but placed themselves within the identity of being mobile.
Their very mobility provided a way of classifying Quakers,
and they were accused of vagrancy and known as itinerants.
They moved away from fixed geographical categorization so
that their arrival elsewhere could only be expected, strangers
whose arrival was foretold: Fox's journeys 'produce repeated
arrivals, new or renewed encounters, in new or revisited
places' (Hinds 2011, p. 117).

When the Quaker Francis Howgill wrote in 1662 of his experience in the early Quaker movement that he knew 'a place to
stand in and what to wait in' (*Quaker Faith and Practice* 1995:
19.08), he was not talking about a geographical place but a
spiritual state of being. When Howgill used the term 'place', he
was referring to the new space of divine intimacy with God.

> The Kingdom of Heaven did gather us and catch us all, as
> in a net, and his heavenly power at one time drew many
> hundreds to land. We came to know a place to stand in
> and what to wait in; and the Lord appeared daily to us,
> to our astonishment, amazement and great admiration . . .

And from that day forward, our hearts were knit unto the Lord and one unto another in true and fervent love, in the covenant of Life with God; and that was a strong obligation or bond upon all our spirits, which united us one unto another. We met together in the unity of the Spirit, and of the bond of peace, treading down under our feet all reasoning about religion. (Ibid.)

The whole of creation became a 'place' for Quakers and their itinerancy signalled and embodied this call. Because personal encounter was so crucial to the Quaker witness, walking also facilitated and signalled the holy potential of all people everywhere. It also symbolized what Fox called 'trampling all that is contrary under' (*Quaker Faith and Practice* 1995: 19.32). He walked 'over the world' (ibid.) not in the sense of passing across its surface but in the sense of walking on top of, and treading under, 'the worldly': the practices of the ungodly and apostate (those who have fallen from the faith). Walking symbolized and constituted holy living. Hinds comments that as speech gives way to silence, so walking gave way to stillness (2011, p. 119). Walking was the interval between human and divine encounter, but it was also Fox's mode of faithfulness.

Jon Kershner's work on John Woolman, eighteenth-century American Quaker tailor and prophetic minister, highlights a similar but distinct relationship between travel and faith (2011, 2012). Like Fox, Woolman travelled extensively.

As an adult, Woolman would travel as far south as North Carolina, north into Massachusetts, west into the Pennsylvania frontier, and east to England where he died in York in 1772. All in all, Woolman averaged a month per year away from home, but almost 70% of the content of the *Journal* concerns his travels. (Kershner 2011, p. 25)

Under the same kind of direct guidance from God as Fox, Woolman felt compelled to travel and prophesy.

> Woolman made more than thirty religious journeys as a Quaker minister. On these journeys he expressed a wide variety of critiques of 18th Century British North American culture ranging from the use of silver dinnerware to lotteries to imperial expansion, to slavery, to the mistreatment of coach horses and post boys. He developed a prophetic voice that called Quakers, and society as a whole, toward just dealings with the oppressed. However, these were not disparate concerns. All of these criticisms were united in Woolman's overarching belief that 'Christ's government' was being established directly on earth and humanity was called to faithfully partner with God in working toward the full establishment of God's rule. (Ibid.)

The difference between Fox and Woolman is that Fox often had openings *after* walking, whereas Woolman claimed he had a greater insight into what God was calling him to do when he was on the road. Away from everyday routine and the mediating influences of his regular company, Woolman experienced the presence of God all the more clearly: travelling opened Woolman to divine revelation (Kershner 2011, p. 27). His travels corresponded to a process of personal transformation while also allowing him to spread new-found insights among those he encountered, thus aiding their spiritual formation (ibid.). Travel, then, was key to new wisdom. God told Woolman to travel in order to be able to guide him further along his spiritual path: 'Woolman believed that the physical act of travel, on one hand, and divine revelation, on the other hand, were mutually reinforcing dynamics' (Kershner 2012).

> [T]he physical motion of itinerant ministry paralleled Woolman's 'spiritual itinerary', which Woolman believed culminated in a state of union to divine love . . . Woolman understood the act of travel itself to be a counter-cultural embodiment of God's absolute rule over all human affairs. (Kershner 2011, p. 24)

Contrary to Fox's experience, then, walking was not the interval but the means of discernment and witness. Travel was part of their call or vocation for both men but there are two major differences between Fox and Woolman. Firstly, Fox's walking was a prelude to an encounter whereas for Woolman it was an end in itself: the journey embodied the encounter. For us in our spiritual lives, either approach to faithfulness might be true. Secondly, Woolman returned home after travelling, while Fox travelled without a definite sense of any one place as home. I explore this second theme more in the next section. The point I wish to end this section with, however, is that both men travelled as a way of being faithful. They did only what they had been told to do. Their travel was purely an act of faith.

Motion and Stability

George Fox was itinerant most of his life, and even when he married Margaret Fell in 1669, he was hardly ever 'home'. John Woolman, on the other hand, regularly had to discern whether or not, and when, to leave his family. By Woolman's time, Quakerism had moved away from some of its earlier certainties. Indeed Woolman is unusual for an eighteenth-century Quaker in the way that he speaks with the confidence and prophetic edge similar to the first Quakers. In the place of a movement based in itinerant preaching, eighteenth-century Quakerism had developed a hierarchy of local, regional and

annual 'Meetings' and a highly bureaucratic internal organization. This structure did not diminish the primary authority of experience but individual leadings needed to be 'tested'
against corporate experience: only those released by a 'minute'
of the 'Meeting' could travel as a Quaker minister. Hundreds
of Quakers throughout the eighteenth and nineteenth centuries were 'released' to travel in the ministry in order to help
spread their spiritual insights to as many Quakers as possible (Stevens 2013). Direct personal experience was comple-
mented by the mediating influence of those whose experience
had been most profound. The stable organization funded and
governed the scale and scope of itinerancy: greater stability
among the movement meant greater regulation of mobility
(the normative governing the extra-ordinary).

Such a shift of emphasis from life as travel, to life being
based in stability is key to an understanding of the commodification of travel, and in turn its potential secularization. When
I was seventeen, I cycled to India. This journey showed me
how the purpose of life is so tied to its mode. I carried tools,
maps, a change of clothes, a sawn-off toothbrush, and most
critically, paper. Toilet paper and paper to write on. Whereas
backpackers and motor-born travellers often head from town
to town and meet and re-meet in hostels and train stations
and bus depots, the long-distance budget cycle-tourist travels
from the middle of nowhere to the middle of nowhere. Every
night I would ask a farmer if I could camp for one night only
and that all I needed was water. I had a lightweight tent and
sleeping bag that took up very little space, and a small camping stove that ran off methylated spirits. I returned to England
after seven months of having lived out of a few small bags.
Mike Carter, who cycled around the coast of Britain, writes:
'Daily life on a long-distance bike trip seemed to be reduced
to the core constituents: physical effort, food for fuel, finding
shelter. Simple. Blissful' (2012, p. 96). On my journey, the

purpose of my life for that time had been to travel and I had needed very little to do it. Pure travelling requires only what we need for the journey. Peace Pilgrim (1908–81) walked 25,000 miles across North America in the cause of peace, without money or possessions. Patterns of consumption can be very lean. The point of this kind of travelling is to travel. The purpose of life is travel and therefore we only need take with us that which helps us do so.

When we wish to create, we tend to need more. To write, we need a pen and paper. If we are to stay in one place, we might prefer a table to write on and after a time perhaps our own dwelling, rather than simply commuting between tent and the public library. We may get tired of using the forest as our toilet, and regular showers may become more important as our lives cease to be tied to the road. Without travelling filling the day, we may want to engage in other activities. We may be in a place with electric light and not sleep 14 hours on winter nights. If we decide to do paid work, we may then rent a place to stay more regularly and we then need to buy clothes to work in. We might start to develop a more settled life, enjoy the creation of others, such as the cinema or theatre or meals out. Today, for example, I have more than one bicycle as I have a 'home', where I can store them. We buy furniture and an oven, instead of using just a camping stove. We have a range of pans and utensils. We can now create food on grander scale and we can play Jenga with the washing up instead of cleaning the single pan-plate of the cycle journey. We may use a car to take ourselves to places and back again quickly and bring purchases back home. Once installed into a fixed location, we buy more stuff to keep the house and garden in order, books to read at moments of leisure or music to listen to and something to listen to it on. The home, a private space, creates a desire for private convenience – our own computer, our own washing machine, personal belongings rather than shared or borrowed ones. Life is no longer just about the onward journey but is instead about the creative potential afforded by stability and the stuff we accumulate to help make that happen more comfortably. To combine the two is not easy. Travelling barbers or circus acts need more than a bicycle to take all they need.

Thus, when those of us with stable home lives travel, we are usually leaving home with a plan to return. We take only what we need for the journey, the destination, the time 'away'. From my more settled lifestyle, I take for three weeks in the USA far more than I took for seven months of cycling. I take with me not only more clothes and more toiletries but also the means to continue creating 'on the road', perhaps books to teach from or a computer to write on and e-mail with. The travel sits alongside the rest of life, rather than being the mode of life. It is a way of trying to do both, travel (as the work requires) and work (when the travel ceases). In this sense, the journey itself is the deviant behaviour. It is unusual. Even for Woolman, he did not undertake his journeys lightly, and he needed to prepare for them. Travel becomes the interruption to stability, the additional activity to everyday life.

To travel continually, we disengage from a stable life. To travel occasionally, we need to engage the means to travel. When the journey is the interruption, it and its components become liable to commodification. When travel is added on to a stable life rather than replacing it, we turn to others to buy what we need to 'go'.

As modernity has become obsessed with the efficient commodification of time, we in turn run our stable lives by the clock, frightened to 'lose time', 'waste time' or 'run out of time'. Punishment is to 'do [only] time'. The sense of finitude leads to an anxiety about being where we need to be at the right time, including whether we have achieved all we wanted to before the moment of our death (Fenn 1995). The secular version is the 'bucket list', the list of all we wish to have done before we die or 'kick the bucket'. Our desire to travel is often accompanied by an anxiety about the time we have in which to do it. When mass travel became affordable with the advent of the railway, agency around time also became critical. Buying time, either by the means to speed travel up or by the need not to work, was initially the domain of the rich, until fast travel became more widely affordable or disposable income more widely spread as a phenomenon.

If our time is limited, we may need to buy time in the form of speed to get from A to B, such as trains or aeroplanes. If the journey is more than a daily commute, we need to buy temporary accommodation, and we may need to buy special clothes or equipment for the journey, such as luggage to carry the clothes. Critically, we may not need to own any of these things, we simply need the use of them to facilitate our intermission from the everyday. We don't need to own the plane or even the car, but we buy space on the plane or rent a car. We don't need to own an apartment elsewhere but rent one or a hotel room or guest-house room. We may not want to own skis, just hire some.

Once the potential of demand and supply is established, those supplying use marketing to co-opt our interest in such things as consumers, and we are offered transport, accommodation and destinations we may not even have imagined, presented in the most alluring ways. Specific destinations, and specific means of getting there, are all sold. We can even buy advice on choosing our 'holiday capsule wardrobe', the clothes we will need to buy and take just for this excursion. 'Packages' gather together our different needs (and perhaps more) into a single purchase for convenience and, we trust, seamless cohesion. As our disposable income increases, our travel plans may become more adventurous or more exotic. They may become more frequent or for shorter periods of time. We can afford more speed or more distance.

As our travel intermits with the regularities of life, it also becomes more public. We tell our neighbours we are going away or tell our colleagues what it was like once we are back. Our travel is displayed not only by our departure and return but by the stories we tell and the photographs we show after the event. Our destinations become public knowledge, eliciting tales from others who have also been there and who can now vicariously join in our travelogue, or questions from those who aspire to one day do what we have just done. It is difficult to go away and not talk about it, such is the social curiosity of those around us, particularly when their stability of having a certain pool of friends and acquaintances around them has been disturbed by our ripple of travel. Our travel denotes status in that it has required an excess of income over subsistence expenditure. Now that most of us can afford at least some holiday, the destination or the accommodation or even how we got there becomes the primary item of 'display travel'. Expensive luxury transport such as the Venice Orient Express or renting a Bentley or travelling by cruise liner may feature more in accounts of the journey than the destination.

Some of us parade our journeys for those left behind as the latest 'display purchase'. As with any other commodity, hierarchies develop and we can find ourselves negotiating our place on the ladder. In any pubic setting, we can hear people swapping stories of destinations and hotels, food and fares. Just the other day, I heard two strangers get into a conversation on a train which included: 'I'm not a conventional traveller, I don't believe in sitting on beaches', and 'I've just been to the Taj Mahal – it's got to be done, hasn't it'. Such 'display tales' often masquerade as advice as the voice of experience can run off a series of encounters with different airlines or different routes to a range of destinations. We can often tell what the speaker's motivation is by reflecting on whether or not we asked for the advice in the first place. Faced with an earlier version of such exchanges, Vita Sackville-West commented that travel should be 'the most private of pleasures. There is no greater bore than the travel bore' (Sackville-West 2007, p. 25).

Travel, when added to lives of stability, potentially becomes a commodity. We buy it and we use it. We consume and rarely interpret our daily travels as part of a spiritual call in our lives. The fact that travel has become so normative masks this aspect of our journeys. We do not always see how optional a purchase it is, and also how its modern framing is so far removed from the vocational pulls and pushes of those Scriptural figures or the early Quakers mentioned above. I look next at the secularizing tendencies of how we have come to travel.

The Framing of Modern Travel

The Grand Tour, the standard educational enhancement for the young elite between 1660 and the 1820s (when steam travel made such journeys more affordable and thus 'cheapened' their appeal) was felt to both educate the traveller and upon their return educate those who could read their accounts. Thus personal formation and the passing on of insight mirrored in some ways the Quaker practice of travelling in the ministry. However, as C. John Somerville notes, belief in providence began to wane towards the end of the seventeenth century, to be replaced by a greater belief in the authority of human agency (1992, p. 3). Spiritual empiricism, as we find in early Quakerism, was replaced in this case by a cultural one, the belief being that sensory exposure to fine art and architecture could culturally educate the young elites sufficiently to take up the positions of leadership they would assume (Buzard 2002, p. 38). A governor or tutor took over the role of the Divine in terms of instruction and the route was a fairly standard one (ibid.). The young elite would travel from England to Paris, where they would learn French, the cultural language of the ruling classes in Europe at the time, and how to fence or ride. Then they would travel on to Switzerland and Italy, perhaps returning via northern Europe. It could take many months or years. James Buzard, scholar of travel writing in the eighteenth and nineteenth centuries, claims that the Grand Tour represented a new paradigm of travelling that was to be superseded by mass tourism (2002, p. 37). The aim of the Grand Tour was ideological and political rather than spiritual, and its virtues and destinations shaped the Cook's Tour which was to eclipse it. In this, we can see how the dawn of mass tourism was borne on the back of a secularized educational itinerary rather than one based on obedience to the Divine. As Buzard notes, as the years since the English Reformation increased, so the Protestant elite stayed in Rome with greater ease and even appreciation (p. 40). Both motivation and agency were secular in comparison with the preaching visits of Quaker ministers, even if the travellers held a personal faith: those travelling bought this form of travel because they wanted to, not because God instructed them to.

The same was true of the popular travel that was to follow in the wake of the Grand Tour. However ardent Thomas Cook's own faith was, his excursions were designed to be morally improving rather than spiritually transforming. As mass tourism took over from elite travel in the nineteenth century, its framing was already secular.

Thomas Cook organized his first excursion aged 32. The date was Monday, 5 July 1841.

[I]n the morning a large body of excursionists, variously numbered at 570 and 485, gathered at Leicester station. They were accompanied by temperance officers and a uniformed brass band, and watched by a crowd some two or three thousand strong. Marshalled by Cook, they climbed on board one second-class carriage and nine 'tubs', the open, seatless carriages in which third-class passengers travelled during the early days of rail, and set off on the eleven mile journey. Every bridge along the line was thronged with spectators and when the train arrived in Loughborough, it was greeted by a crush of temperance supporters and onlookers. (Brendon 1991, p. 6)

Lunch was provided in the park by Cook, then the group returned to the station to meet groups from Derby, Nottingham and Harborough. Together they wandered around town, sang the Teetotal National Anthem in the Market Square and then went back to the park for a spoken grace, tea, games, and speeches, the day ending at 9pm. It was a day of celebrating its own success and pleasure. At one point, Cook cried out: 'One more cheer, for Teetotalism and Railwayism!!!' (Brendon 1991, p. 8). He was not the first organizer of excursions but this day was still 'a startling novelty' (p. 12) and Cook was definitely a pioneer. He was able to utilize the advantages of the new railway system over the slower and less comfortable stagecoaches that had preceded it. Cook claimed: 'Railway travelling is travelling for the million' (p. 16).

The railway meant that certain towns, like Brighton, became resorts or destinations. Moving from places which were initially sold for their health benefits, seaside towns quickly developed into popular leisure resorts (Shields 1991, pp. 82, 110–11). They developed what Rob Shields has called 'place-myths' (p. 109), where location and social imagination collaborate to create popular conceptualizations, malleable and contestable, but also persistent. Urry uses the concept to identify one of the ways the Lake District was made into a tourist destination of a particular kind (1995, p. 194) and shows how places take on their own cultural capital, their own particular patterns of tourist consumption, e.g. rock in Blackpool, ginger-bread in Grasmere. Each place derived its own brand of secu-larized tourist 'pilgrimage'. The place was consumed in terms of services and goods as well as enthusiasm. Two forces came together: the material development of locations for tourism and the entrepreneurial abilities of those who helped attract and bring the people to them.

In the 1860s, Thomas Cook and his son John Mason Cook expanded their business to include trips to the continent. Brendon claims Cook 'helped to domesticate Switzerland': 'By making Switzerland more comfortable, Cook contrived to make it less exotic' and 'turned what had once been an adven-ture into an institution' (Brendon 1991, p. 82). Commentators like John Ruskin were appalled at the attitude of the new trav-ellers as they consumed these foreign grounds. For Ruskin, nowhere they went was unspoilt. There appeared to him to be no:

> foreign city in which the spread of your presence is not marked among its fair old streets and happy gardens by a consuming white leprosy of new hotels and perfumers' shops: the Alps themselves, which your own poets used to love so reverently, you look upon as soaped poles in a bear garden, which you set yourself to climb and slide down again with 'shrieks of delight'. (Ruskin 2002, p. 53)

By 1911, 55 percent of the population of England and Wales had at least one week by the sea each year (Urry 2002, p. 18). The growth of institutionalized holidays for the working classes into week-long holidays, wakes weeks, became standard in order to achieve a greater reliability of production in the other 51 weeks. In 1950, a million Britons went abroad (Brendon 1991, p. 292). Today, 'holiday' has become disassociated from its etymological root of being a holy-day. Indistinct from any other part of life, we see a holiday as part of regular life (Urry 1995, p. 130). Perhaps 'inter-rail' or the 'gap year' between school and University became the 'grand tour' of secular modernity, democratized albeit with a different set of sites to visit. Those of us who want to avoid the 'shrieks of delight' of mass appeal need to find quieter places of retreat in more remote locations, or stay at home.

The Romance of Travel

Accounts of the Grand Tour romanticized the notion of travel, of all it could provide, and its very process too. As the Grand Tour was an exercise in the authority of cultural knowledge, so the romance of modern travel has been constructed through a parallel popular discourse of music, film and book. There have always been songs about travel. Modern examples include Gene Pitney's 'Twenty Four Hours from Tulsa' and 'The Long and Winding Road' by The Beatles. The genre of 'road trip movie' is a recent addition to the huge wealth of travel literature, accounts and guides that allow us either vicarious pleasures of others' travels or allow us to plan and predict our next moves. The 1936 film *Night Mail*, complete with W. H. Auden poem and music by Benjamin Britten, celebrated the technology of travel that allowed letters to move from London to Glasgow for delivery while the rest of us slept. Patrick Holland and Graham Huggan claim that the travel book, as commodity, in turn commodifies travel (1998, p. 198). Travel is romanticized as a noble activity, one of consequence, and in and of itself technologically or geographically exciting.

I find travel romantic because it has been presented to me as such. Bicycle, motorcycle and car magazines all feature their wares in delicious settings and tell of wondrous journeys on or in beautiful machines. The raison d'être for these machines is that they move. Therefore, they are presented in idyllic else-wheres, where we are led to believe that we too could go if we only had the same means. Having said that, the idea of the travel is often more exciting than the reality of the travel itself. Crossing water in a huge ferry is a wonderful idea for me but the constant churning of the engine, inclement weather, and over-priced food usually make me very glad when it is over. Plotting the line on the map may be more exciting than the experience of travelling the line.

If I think of 'romantic journeys' I have made, journeys whose memory evokes a sense of mystery and excitement associated with the love of travel, they might include: midnight bus con-voys from London to Glasgow; crossing America by coach; hot-air balloon journeys; crossing Saudi Arabia by juggernaut; sailing in the Arabian Ocean; motorcycling around Tanzania or Sri Lanka; outback journeys in Australia; and travelling from Carlisle to Bombay by bicycle.

This romanticization is, I suggest, imagination-driven. The night-time bus journey could be anywhere; it is the lights of the cities that are exciting to me in their pattern and for the mys-tery that lies behind them. The four-day bus journey across the States is not about the scenery, it is about the fulfilment of living in the same kind of world Jack Kerouac wrote about. Elsewhere, the dreams can be technological (as in riding in a hot-air balloon or the juggernaut with its wonderful seats, great height and crowd of dials and switches) or geographical as in exploring parts of the globe that I never imagined I would see. Motorcycling anywhere is fun; perhaps overcoming adversity on small machines adds the element of the unknown, of not knowing what may come next. Certainly the longer trips are liable to forces beyond our control and this 'pure travel' where the timetabling is most loose allows us the excitement of not knowing what will happen next and the challenge of overcom-ing the unforeseen. On my seven-month bicycle trip, there were no fixed points and days spent haggling for visas were equal to days spent cycling. It was all about completing the journey. Journeys become romantic, when we make them so.

Alain de Botton, in his *The Art of Travel* (2002) describes his romantic constructions of travel. He finds the colours and patterns made by the lights of night-time traffic poetic: 'traffic ran in silent, elegant symmetry along six lanes, the differences in makes and colours of cars disguised by the gathering darkness leaving a uniform ribbon of red and white diamonds extending into infinity in two directions' (2002, pp. 31–2). It reminds him of '[o]ther equally and unexpectedly poetic travelling places – airport terminals, harbours, train stations, and motels' (ibid.). Whereas for me, the long-distance truck stop or service station is a romantic site, de Botton travels to Heathrow to see the planes leave and land when he is feeling sad: 'As every ship turns into a gate, a choreographed dance begins' (p. 37). People come off, used blankets and pillows are exchanged, fuel and food replaced, luggage extracted, engines maintained.

> Nowhere is the appeal of the airport more concentrated than in the television screens which hang in rows from terminal ceilings announcing the departure and arrival of flights and whose absence of aesthetic self-consciousness, whose workmanlike casing and pedestrian typefaces, do nothing to disguise their emotional charge or imaginative allure. (de Botton 2002, p. 39)

For de Botton, this perpetual sense of possibility, of going somewhere–anywhere where no one knows our names, is uplifting. I am reminded of the clickety-clack of the rolling letters on departure boards at railway stations. At Philadelphia 30th Street Station, complete with its huge 1950 Walter Hancock statue of the 'Angel of the Resurrection' acting like a guardian over all who travel, passengers rush (outwardly and inwardly) to form a line whenever a platform is announced.

De Botton also likes aeroplane take-offs: 'The display of power can inspire us to imagine analogous, decisive shifts in our own lives; to imagine that we too might one day surge above much that looms over us' (2002, p. 41). Flight has magic for him as 'the road' does for me. De Botton idealizes even in-flight catering: 'With the in-flight tray, we make ourselves at home in this unhomely place; we appropriate the extraterrestrial landscape with the help of a chilled bread roll and a plastic tray of potato salad' (p. 45). There is for him a delight of being 'elsewhere' – an exotic language, an unusual font on a sign, electrical socket or currency. As John Urry states about when we travel, we become semioticians, readers of meaning in all we see (ibid.). We can find 'fit' or not, depending on what suits us. Do we see a scary chaos on the roads in Cairo with cars going both ways round a roundabout or a vibrant creativity? We choose and interpret our travel and construct what we find special accordingly rather than be guided by the Divine.

De Botton talks of what John Urry calls the 'romantic gaze', a quiet undisturbed moment in the Lake District (2002, p. 155), the memory of which comes back later to ease anxieties on a busy day in London. Travel gives us a capital of having been elsewhere, an arsenal of memories that can help us break with routine and with work, a displaced sense of travel. We remember what we want to and fuel the romantic imagination as we plan our next foray.

Nowadays, some of us travel even to celebrate travel. St Louis airport is a shrine for those who wish to celebrate the first transatlantic flight. Car museums celebrate past attempts to travel in comfort and style and lure present owners of these older cars to their doors. Often redundant as vehicles for general use, it is interesting that part of the function of classic car magazines is to help owners find excuses to drive their cars *somewhere* by listing potential destinations such as these museums. Complex romantic ideals confront me as I read these magazines. I loved the waft and dip of my Bentley, perfect for London, as I could never drive very far given the traffic, thus never really punished by its wicked fuel consumption. I loved the graceful anonymity of my Bristol or the way I could push an Austin Seven or Citroen 2CV around a garage forecourt. The vehicles themselves, the means of motion, have their own delights and connotations. Boys can fulfil the aspiration to become like train drivers in their very own cars!

For 'petrolheads', Jack Kerouac's *On the Road* remains a definitive classic. Kerouac's narrator Sal Paradise tells the story of Dean Moriarty, unsettled traveller criss-crossing the USA, and how the road and 'heading elsewhere' becomes the stable constant of home. For Dean, to travel is to live life to the full: 'The road is life' (1972, p. 199).

At one point, Dean and Sal, sitting in the back of a car as hitchhikers, distinguish between themselves as pure travellers able to face whatever is given them, as opposed to those in the front of the car concerned with where to stay a few hours ahead. Dean says:

> Now you just dig them in front. They have worries, they're counting the miles, they're thinking about where to sleep tonight, how much money for gas, the weather, how they'll get there – and all the time they'll get there anyway, you see. But they need to worry and betray time with urgencies false and otherwise, purely anxious and whiny, their souls really won't be at peace unless they can latch on to an established and proven worry and having once found it they assume facial expressions to fit and go with it, which is, you see, unhappiness, and all the time it all flies past them and they know it and that *too* worries them no end. (Kerouac 1972, pp. 196–7)

Dean and Sal contrast their own assured sense of pure travel with the anxiety of those concerned about where they are going and whether they will get all they 'should' out of such a trip. Those in the front are not open to 'the road' but are always in their heads with worry, and really wanting to be home. Their anxiety sets them apart from the reader who identifies with Sal's and Dean's sense of travel as normative. In our identification with the text, we too differentiate ourselves from the anxious travellers and are led to embrace the celebration and romanticization of travel.

In 1986, my journey across the USA echoed those of Sal Paradise and Dean Moriarty. I travelled from Philadelphia to San Francisco by bus to spend 60 hours there, to return and head back to New York to fly home. I had no car, no companions, but I was *on the road*. I had a Trailways bus pass, and all of America was mine. However, when the bus timetables changed on Labor Day, it meant I would not make my flight home. I was left to panhandle around Denver bus station to buy another ticket with another company. Denver, so central to the journeyings in *On the Road*, became a key location for me too. I shared that need with Sal and Dean to get out, in my case to get 'back'. Finally, I begged the price of a ticket for a Greyhound Bus that would get me to New York on time. I got away and felt again what Kerouac called the 'purity of the road' (1972, p. 128).

It was a time of freedom. The freedom of youth, or rather the freedom a lack of stability or responsibility gives us. In spite of having a flight home on a particular day, I was still in a time of pure travel rather than managed itinerancy. Only the need for income betrays the ability to wander, and yet it is this income which then allows us to travel again, even if it is in rationed amounts. In the book, Dean Moriarty's father travelled to New Mexico for the winter (1972, p. 255). He moved towns in order to stay warm instead of using technology to keep a single location temperate. Migration or central heating and cooling is a choice. The rich of course, 'snow-birds', can do both.

Towards the end of the book, Dean and Sal reach Mexico. It seems like a perfect destination.

> We gazed and gazed at our wonderful Mexican money that went so far, and played with it and looked around and smiled at everyone. Behind us lay the whole of America and everything Dean and I had previously known about life, and life on the road. We had finally found the magic land at the end of the road and we never dreamed the extent of the magic. '*Think* of these cats staying up all hours of the night,' whispered Dean. 'And think of this big continent ahead of us with those enormous Sierra Madre mountains we saw in the movies, and the jungles all the way down and a whole desert plateau as big as ours and reaching clear down to Guatemala and God knows where, whoo! What'll we do? What'll we do? Let's move!' We got out and went back to the car. One last glimpse of America across the hot lights of the Rio Grande bridge, and we turned our back and fender to it and roared off. (Kerouac 1972, p. 259)

Even at the end of the rainbow, the instinct is to keep moving. The end of the road is the start of the next one: 'I want to get on and on – this road drives *me!!*' (1972, p. 263). It is always more interesting ahead, they claim.

Sal continually notices those places or people left behind receding until they become dispersed specks: 'It was sad to see his tall figure receding in the dark as we drove away, just like other figures in New York and New Orleans: they stand uncertainly underneath immense skies, and everything about them is drowned' (1972, p. 158). Elsewhere, 'And Denver receded back of us like the city of salt, her smokes breaking up in the air and dissolving to our sight' (p. 252). At the end of the book, Dean Moriarty is the receding figure left at a street corner as

Sal heads off in a car never to see him again. This book was one of my bibles, when I was seventeen. It hinted at all I thought I wanted – travel, speed, 'digging' the world. Now such a life feels less alluring and charming. As happened to its hero over the course of the book, the lure of continually-never-stopping palled. The thrill receded. What we find exciting changes and our romanticization of travel, constructed as it is, is unlikely to remain constant.

Travel in a Secular World

Seeing our holiday travel as indistinct from the rest of life or constructing certain aspects of travel as romantic are not inherently secular processes. We might, like Francis Howgill, know 'a place to stand in' and find everything, even our imagination, has been brought under a spiritual canopy. Even our romantic instincts may possibly be fed by the spiritual. However, in general, our sense of self has shifted so that we now feel able to make our own decisions. Most of us no longer attribute everything to the spiritual realm and no longer wish to consult divine guidance for every decision. Sociologists of religion like Bryan Wilson (1982) and Steve Bruce (2011) have characterized the decline in the salience and presence of religion and spirituality within public life in terms of what is referred to as the 'secularization thesis'. For anyone interested in the state of religion of Britain, it is a well-rehearsed picture. While levels of religious belief remain fairly high, church attendance has dropped generation by generation. Bruce argues that modernist individualism has turned us into consumers of religion. At the same time, the proliferation of religious groups which have replaced the canopy of the state Church, leads to a fragmentation of 'communal conceptions of the moral and supernatural order' (2011, p. 31). We no longer all believe the same things and the existence of competing claims gives each claim less authority, and makes religious transmission diffuse or implausible. Welfare roles such as poor relief, previously monopolized by the Church, have been taken over by the State, thus weakening the role of the Church in everyday life. Technological advance means we have less recourse to religion, and our increased economic stability and ability to fix what is broken means that we are less likely to pray for help. Modernist faith is privatized and compartmentalized and individualized and we are far less likely to go to church than we used to. Seven per cent of us in Britain attend church weekly. We live in a secular society where choice based on our own authority is seen as valid and 'natural'. Our excitements and desires, including those regarding travel, are no longer tied to a sense of calling or vocation.

There is the idea, expressed by David Lodge's fictional academic Rupert Sheldrake in *Paradise News* (1991), that in our secular society, tourism has replaced pilgrimage, and that tourism represents a secularized version of the holy journey. He relates: 'The thesis of my book is that sightseeing is a substitute for religious ritual. The sightseeing tour as secular pilgrimage. Accumulation of grace by visiting the shrines of high culture. Souvenirs as relics. Guidebooks as devotional aids' (1991, p. 75). More than this, I suggest, all our travel today, not just tourism, is framed within the processes of secularization. When we are the agents of travel, both in its motivation and its realization, our travel is not explicitly connected to the spiritual realm.

In the way that religious conviction has become compartmentalized and relativized, so 'pure travel' has become packaged and rationed out into competing options for us as consumers. Few of us can travel all the time and so we buy 'approximations' of our dream expeditions. We opt in and out of being away, as time and money permit. We choose to take a day trip to the seaside or book an escorted six-month journey. Most

crucially, we have an increased ability to indulge our own preferences for travel. We have the financial and intellectual means,
have become our own agents and only need buy the help we
decide we want, the flight but not the package, the hire car but
not the hotel. We decide when and where we want to go and
we can find someone who can help us get there. We don't feel
we need a spiritual seal of approval.

Everywhere is now a potential destination; 'anywhere' is
seen as equally 'away'. Travel is mediated by the market, differentiated by different needs and niches, serviced by series
of specialists. Some locations/destinations and routes there
and back become highly managed and in turn presented and
re-presented as attractive holiday destinations. This builds
desire and anticipation and often popularity. Everywhere,
even our home town, can be sold as someone else's potential
exotic location. Pubs never frequented by locals are remem-
bered as 'finds' to travellers in search of lunch.

Romance may rarely enter enforced or constrained travel but
with agency and income, we can buy into our dreams rather
than our spiritual leadings. Romantic notions of travel are secular mirrors of spiritual call. Based often on our own desires,
rather than divine prompting, we opt for particular types of
time away from the everyday. They may be remote, they may
be distinct from our daily routines or they may fulfil ambitions.
We may travel by particular means or to particular locations.
If we are really lucky, our daily commute may be such a bene-
diction. At the end of the day, most of us manage our own
stability and travel, and travel led by a sense of spiritual call is
unusual these days.

Now, even pilgrimages are sold as packages. Journeys with
a holy intent are sold in convenient forms and marketed in the
same way as holidays. We can buy a trip to Lourdes, or Taizé,
or book a deluxe Haj or Umrah package. We can combine piety
with en-suite luxury. On the Camino (the path which leads to

Santiago del Compostela), as the pilgrimage has become popular, there are tales of 'pilgrims' who carve their initials into trees, offend local sensibilities by walking in bikinis or drop their litter along the way. The process of pilgrimage is lost as we behave like holiday makers: for some of us, destination has become more important than journey. The Camino has been commodified and the consequences are clear.

In the Quaker setting, where the word 'pilgrimage' might be seen as anathema to a group which counts all space as equally sacred, the '1652 country' has developed its own routinized itineraries to ease the passage of the many groups of Quakers from all over the world who wish to retrace George Fox's footsteps. Historian Angus Winchester has shown that since 1952, the 300th anniversary of those heady months, the language of 'pilgrimage' has become embedded in the Quaker popular consciousness:

> Despite George Fox's insistence that the so-called consecrated ground of a steeple house was no more holy than any other ground, Quakers do have their own 'holy places', notably the sites in north-west England, spread out across northern Lancashire and southern Cumbria, which were associated with the electrifying events of Fox's encounter with the Westmoreland Seekers in 1652. As a result, the names of Pendle Hill, Swarthmoor, Brigflatts, and Firbank are firmly embedded in the corporate Quaker consciousness and have been borrowed to name schools and colleges, and other Quaker institutions on both sides of the Atlantic. (Winchester 1993, p. 373)

Quakers can now buy a place on a weekend pilgrimage. It is not just commercialism. For the Quakers on these trips, the history begins to carry greater meaning. Such organized tours make the destinations accessible and offer all the convenience of the single-purchase package. Some are run by charities rather than for profit and even those earning their living this way may see this income simply as way of being 'released for their ministry'. However, I am more concerned about how the selling of such trips turns pilgrims into consumers. Do we start ticking off the holy shrines as others tick off their wish-list of destinations? Do we now 'do' Lourdes as we 'do' Bali? Are we are in danger of 'buying' travel with a specifically religious dimension in a manner akin to any other purchase? In a secularizing society, where organized religion has a diminished salience in our everyday lives, how far do we discern what it is we are to buy?

James Clifford in *Routes: Travel and Translation in the Late Twentieth Century* talks of the centuries of human propensity to movement as 'dwelling in travel' (1997, p. 2). For Clifford, we dwell within a normative mode of travel. No longer is travel represented by the major moment of departure but routinized and concealed within daily or annual schedules. Travel has become so normative in our everyday lives that we can travel unconsciously. That does not mean we travel mystically without recourse to rational thought, but that we do not realize that every journey is an act and a choice. Our increased ability to travel, the fact that we can be authors of our own journeys now that we may have private transport, and our anxiety about running out of time collude to make us travel without thinking. We become not only the author of itineraries but the authors of our own leadings. Are we led by 'God' or by our own preferences? It is interesting, as John Knox found in a study of church life in Oregon, that even among those of us who still attend church, we tend to choose those settings which most affirm our own ideas (2009). Even within our spiritual life, we become our own authorities, a phenomenon Knox calls 'sacro-egoism' (ibid.). Maybe we have travel-egoism too.

The American Quaker teacher and writer Rufus Jones told a joke about a man given an allotment in the 1920s. It was a very poor piece of land, full of weeds and very unpromising.

The man tilled it and tilled it and fed it and finally produced a fantastic crop of vegetables. The local minister came along and congratulated him on what he and God had been able to do. 'Thank you,' said the man, 'but you should have seen it when God had it all to himself!' In terms of travel, the joke is on us. We are not making a good job of it. We are travelling too much and harming the planet, and our experience of travel is largely one of discomfort or deprivation. Our ability to look after ourselves and to listen to God or Spirit has not kept pace with our desire to perpetually head elsewhere. As such, our travel rarely affords us the kind of spiritual wisdom John Woolman found, or the kind of time he had to reflect on all he had learnt through his travels. Unlike Fox and Woolman, we neither travel because we are led to, nor do we travel in order to discern. The decision to travel and the experience of travel itself has been, for most of us, highly secularized. More than ever before, we can travel to our heart's desire and our bank balance's capability. We don't need to wait for a vision from God or have a holy purpose to help us go. Leaving and returning is a normal part of life. In short, our lives have become embedded within the ease and allure of modern travel: how can we resist?

2

Trains, Planes and Automobiles

We are caught up within a society of motion. We can travel more than our parents and grandparents ever imagined possible. It is easy and relatively cheap. We can see the fantastical and we can feel enlarged and illuminated by even a weekend expedition. Alain de Botton calls journeys the midwives of thought: 'Few places are more conducive to internal conversations than a moving plane, ship, or train . . . At the end of hours of train-dreaming, we may feel we have been returned to ourselves – that is, brought back into contact with emotions and ideas of importance to us' (2002, p. 57). One friend told me how long train journeys operate for him as a 'rinse cycle', as if he had been placed in a washing machine to come out cleansed at the other end. Our outward travel can deflect and order inward frenzy. We are returned to the everyday less filled with its concerns.

Alongside all the concerns about environment and spiritual enhancement, we can feel our lives enhanced by the possibilities of going somewhere else. These trips are worth saving up for. The difficulty, explored in this chapter, is that our journeys, whether to work or holiday, are often comprised of the same set of challenges and complexities as the life we are trying to rise above. As travel has become consumable, our collective compulsion to travel can represent the very sickness we are trying to escape. Cyclist Mike Carter talks of friends who travel to escape the pressure of work but for whom the trips lack any thrill (2012, p. 106). Much of our travel is a mode of societal dis-ease. Do we suffer a travel sickness of our own making? The journey is often now part of a purchase rather than providence and we are jostled alongside all the other consumers in our attempt to get from A to B.

Bruce Chatwin famously argued that humanity is inherently nomadic and that societal problems begin when we settle down, or become stable in one place:

> We looked up to see a procession of women and children on their way back from foraging. The babies swayed peacefully in the folds of their mothers' dresses. 'You never hear them cry,' Marian said, 'as long as the mother keeps moving.' . . . 'And if babies can't bear to lie still,' I said, 'how shall we settle down later?' (Chatwin 1987, p. 118)

He uses this example of motion being essential for well-being as just one in his argument for mobility as essential. I come back to that idea in my final chapter, but certainly combining travel and stability does not appear to be easy, especially as more and more of us want to go. I focus in this chapter on the experience of the systems of modern travel and how so much of 'travelling well' these days is about managing the discomforts rather than enjoying the experience. The empty road or railway carriage or having three seats on a plane to ourselves are increasingly rare phenomena. Spaciousness in which to enjoy the journey does not come easily or can only be obtained at a huge financial premium. We are often rushed or rushing and travel is not often peaceful. The journey becomes the part of the time away from home to 'get through'. It can become an experience of ordeal rather than ideal. Is it true, as Paul Theroux wrote in *Washington Post*, that 'travel is glamorous only in retrospect'?

Travel as a commodity is no one thing, as it rests partly on where we want to go and how. Cheaper travel may involve merely the means to go from one destination to another, i.e. a bus fare. At the other end of the scale, fully escorted holidays to rare and distant locations, involve far more complex orders of control and management, both of the traveller, and of what they experience. In the following sections, I look at the modern experience of travelling by train, plane and car and how our use of these machines is regulated and ordered to facilitate safe and reliable mass transit. We seek these qualities but they come at a personal cost, a cost that has arisen out of the ease and affordability of travel, indeed the very success of the systems themselves.

The Systematization of the Means of Travel

Travel is highly differentiated today. We have a choice of means of transport, a choice of 'carriers' or 'providers', a choice of comfort levels, a choice of routes, and usually a choice of prices. However, travel is also subject to what George Ritzer termed 'McDonaldization' (1993). McDonaldization has five main features reflecting the way the fast food chain operates, which Ritzer sees as best describing late modern society. They are: efficiency; calculability (or quantifiability of the goal, e.g. 50 hamburgers an hour or a flight to New York carrying 200 passengers); predictability and standardization; control of the processes (e.g. replacing human interaction with non-human resources such as computers); and cultural hybridization, where a dominant cultural model intersects with the local. This reliability of the same product being routinely available has been key to the success of McDonald's restaurants and the other chains that have followed. The same is true of the success of selling travel to so many with such ease. It lay behind the first escorted journeys of Thomas Cook in the 1840s. We have wanted the efficiency, reliability and predictability offered us. Now the escorts may be the resort hosts or the experience of 'there' may be so similar to the one of 'here'

35

that escorts are unnecessary. We want these routinized forms of transport because their familiarity makes us feel safe. The level of risk feels low.

The systems of travel follow regular patterns. Planes and trains and buses leave from the same places at the same times. Timetables do not shift without warning and if they do, we complain. The unexpected delay is the great anxiety of the scheduled traveller. To avoid this, the travel companies themselves demand reliability and repeatability from their suppliers and workforce in order to minimize risk.

Movements on the scale we now enjoy is a product of industrialization, standardization, and differentiation. Bradshaw's railway timetable first appeared in 1839, giving set times when train services would leave for specified destinations. The age of the railway hotel followed, guaranteeing reliable and repeatable levels of accommodation for the weary wanderer. Baedeker guide books were first published in 1829 (Grimshaw 2008, p. 21), offering the visitor information on what to visit and how to view the local setting, how the watcher should see the watched. John Urry builds on Anthony Giddens' work on how social relations have been disembedded from local communities within modernity to explain how travel came to be seen as desirable and so widespread (1995, p. 141). In other words, because we are no longer part of strong local communities, going elsewhere becomes easier. Everywhere, including home, can be enjoyed privately. If we can be private, then everywhere is equally open to being home-like. This involved the establishment of trust-inducing systems of transportation and organization, perhaps exemplified by Thomas Cook and Son. Cook's tours reduced risk, as is the perception of satellite navigation systems. The deskilling is the same in both examples. We lose the need to gain local knowledge (or even read a map), new languages, to experience things first-hand as opposed to having the environment mediated to us by guide or gadget. In this game of not leaving anything to chance, we have put our need above our concern for the environment:

> The history of these repetitive systems is in effect the history of those processes by which the natural world has been 'mastered' and made secure, regulated and relatively risk-free. For people to be able to 'move' and for them in turn to be able to move objects, text, money, water, images, is to establish how it is that nature has been subdued. (Urry, 2011, p. 13)

Huge airport-cities service the travel of others, tens of thousands of workers sort out the million passengers per day. Huge layers of plant and cable, of immobility, transact mobility for us (2011, p. 54). We are both exceptionally free and increasingly dependent on the systems which permit repetition (p. 15). We have laid the industry of travel across the very green fields we have wanted to escape to.

Urry points out the role the computer has come to play in the planning of our journeys; the technology that facilitates our travel, allows us to keep in touch when on the move, and mediates the increasing number of breakdowns of personal and collective journeys (2011, p. 15). We want increased reliability but increased freedom. The dynamic is not an easy one. The mobile phone can only be heralded as an emergency device in a time of so many crises. The more personalized our travel plans, the more complex our work lives, the more we become dislocated from family and community, so we need to rely all the more on such 'bridging technology', to keep in touch, and systems to facilitate mobility.

As part of a mobile society, we take on identities of mobility such as 'leisure-walker', 'train-passenger', 'cycle-rider', what Urry calls 'hybrid geographies' of mode and motion (2011, p. 35). We become a car-driver, not a human driving a car.

Or we become identified by the make of car we drive and join the 'owners' club'. Sociologist Tim Dant has hypothesized the driver-car where the two entities become a single unit (2004): we drive and are driven. In one busy week, I caught four trains to get to Salisbury to teach, then the next day another two to London. I travelled around London by bus and then caught another train to Gatwick. My airport hotel was only a mile away, but the road and security systems of the airport meant that after two hours of trying to walk away from the airport station, I needed in the end to pay for a shuttle bus to take me there. The next day I went south to Haywards Heath and took a second train to London Bridge, a third to Greenwich. I was lucky to be driven back to the hotel. On the fourth day, I got the shuttle to the airport and two trains to Dorking for more teaching, then three trains to Clitheroe. That week, I felt like a rail passenger: so much of my life that week had been about getting the right train from the right platform. In this world on the move, we become our own part of the huge social system of movement.

In *The Little Prince*, the prince meets the railway switchman.

'Good morning,' said the little prince.
'Good morning,' said the railway switchman.
'What do you do here?' the little prince asked.
'I sort out travellers, in bundles of a thousand,' said the switchman. 'I send off the trains that carry them; now to the right, now to the left.'
And a brilliantly lighted express train shook the switchman's cabin as it rushed by with a roar like thunder.
'They are in a great hurry,' said the little prince. 'What are they looking for?'
'Not even the locomotive engineer knows that,' said the switchman.
And a second brilliantly lighted express thundered by, in the opposite direction.
'Are they coming back already?' demanded the little prince.

'These are not the same ones,' said the switchman. 'It is an exchange.'

'Were they not satisfied where they were?' asked the little prince.

'No one is ever satisfied where he is,' said the switchman.

And they heard the roaring thunder of a third brilliantly lighted express.

'Are they pursuing the first travellers?' demanded the little prince.

'They are pursuing nothing at all,' said the switchman. 'They are asleep in there, or if they are not asleep they are yawning. Only the children are flattening their noses against the windowpanes.'

'Only the children know what they are looking for,' said the little prince. 'They waste their time over a rag doll and it becomes very important to them; and if anybody takes it away from them, they cry . . .'

'They are lucky,' the switchman said.

(de Saint-Exupery 1996, pp. 70–1)

The switchman is cynical about why we rush from one place to the next and back again. Ideally, however, we do know, at some level, what we are pursuing as we are moved around. We choose our destinations, our means of motion, and our routes and timing. Hopefully, we get there 'on time' and in one piece. What, though, is our experience of the systems of travel?

Trains

The introduction of the railway collapsed space and time for travellers in a way undreamt of before. Wolfgang Schivelbusch, in his treatise on railway travel, says that with railways, the journey became identified with the destination, rather than the points in between. A place felt closer because it took less time to get there. Schivelbusch says space is 'destroyed' by fast sightless travel (1986, p. 38). The railway was also the driving force behind the standardization of time; in 1880, the railway time became general standard time in Britain (p. 44).

The speed at which trains could travel, in comparison with stage coaches, induced both fear and excitement. Today, even as trains have become quicker, and continue to, we have got used to this speed.

> Travel technologies have often been elevated to core normative status, entire travel cultures taking shape around the vaunted superiority of particular means of transport. In the mid-17th century, coach travel was resisted by some as too 'soft,' whereas 19th-century tastemakers such as John Ruskin contrasted it favorably with the vulgarity of railway transport and claimed that 'all traveling becomes dull in exact proportion to its rapidity'. (Adler 1989, p. 1378)

Indeed, speed can be the main criterion some of us use to decide how to get somewhere else. As we travel further, we want to get there more quickly. We weigh up the option of flying versus the train, and for local journeys, going by car can be quicker and more convenient. In Britain, trains have become the poor relation of our mass transit systems after the Beeching cuts of uneconomic lines in the 1960s, the huge investment in roads, and the denationalization of the railways in the 1980s. We are left with fewer lines to travel, a collage of operators and a reduction in the ability to travel flexibly, with tickets only valid on certain trains or with particular companies. Spontaneity is penalized by higher fares for walk-on travel, reservation systems fail, trains fail and overcrowding is common. 'Quiet coaches' may not be. Long-distance train routes become uneconomic or have a reduced service as planes have become quicker or cheaper alternatives. A journey from Preston to Penzance now takes two or three trains instead of one.

In the 1950s, some of the best chefs worked on the US trains, cooking up amazing delights in full view of the passengers. I am old enough to remember restaurant cars on British trains and how at times, passengers from any part of the train could enjoy its delights. I recall London to St Austell on a Saturday evening, travelling all the way in the restaurant car. That was a sublime journey filled with good food, wonderful views and fine company. Today, trains are often let down by their catering. While major railway stations have been transformed into places of culinary choice, what is available on the trains is limited and often expensive. On my one first-class rail journey, from Clitheroe to Falmouth and back, the 'free' food was rationed on the way down, so that they would have enough for everyone, and had 'gone off' and was therefore unavailable on the way back.

Add more people, indeed fill the train, and the experience is less comfortable, because we are not given enough space to spread out our food and books etc. as we would wish, or we find ourselves worrying about our suitcase crammed in a bulging luggage rack ten seats away from us. We cannot find our reserved seat or we find our cultivated seat turns out to be somebody else's pre-booked one, and we need to move. We need to dislocate our temporary home, relocate, gather up and move on, while all the time being moved through the outside world. Standing up in the speed of the carriage may not be so easy. We may fall into other passengers with our hands too full to steady ourselves. Context is everything as far as enjoyment goes on public transport.

Trains vary too. The high-speed intercity trains are generally plush, have tables, and now come with power outlets, perhaps wifi and food for sale. The local services are sometimes more like buses, often overcrowded, with even less leg room. The '54 minutes past' from Wigan to Manchester Airport is not a romantic beginning to a holiday in paradise, and most of the passengers only travel one or two stops. Travelling on such a train brings to mind the ebb and flow of passengers getting on and getting off. This is a train that actually starts in Southport. I travel on it from Wigan to Bolton. Some may go the whole way, companions to the train crew. A poem, one of many at Wigan Wallgate, posted in the waiting room, reads:

Hopefully I'll get a good seat,
A window seat.
Hopefully I'll miss the rush hour,
Dodge the sleet of my mind.
Somehow escape with daydream
into people's back yards,
the borders of the British rail.
I see the plastic slides and
All that they entail . . .
(Crompton, n. d.)

We want 'good seats' and a lack of rush and rush-hour. We want peace, the ability to escape. We may be lucky and trains, still, are the most reliable means of finding spaciousness when travelling in Britain.

By rail, we travel along the back areas of our cities, the industrial heritage from which the railway was born. Like canal boats, we see a different side to everything than from the window of the car. And we see more. We can walk about, and we are freed from the responsibility of being in charge of motion.

The opportunity and challenge of public transport is that we are given the timetable. This is wonderfully liberating in some ways. When I had a car, there was never any reason not to decline the additional invitation. Going by train, we are squeezed into the timetable but squeezed out of possibility. Now, the timetable and routing of the train and even the restrictions of ticketing free me into a more leisured life. Being given a timetable is also a challenge. I have to leave on time, may need to take a particular train for my ticket to be valid, worry about connections, get fit running with coat and bags, arrive on a train hot and sweaty, or miss the connection and know that even thirty seconds may mean arriving an hour late. If modernity is characterized by an anxiety about time, making a rail connection can be the epitome of such anxiety.

Timetables can involve rushing but they also involve waiting. Damien Galgut sums this up well:

> I wander around and come back, then wander again. A large part of travelling consists purely in waiting, with all the attendant ennui and depression. Memories come back of other places he has waited in, departure halls of airports, bus-stations, lonely kerbsides in the heat, and in all of them there is an identical strain of melancholy summed up in a few transitory details. A paper bag blowing in the wind. The mark of a dirty shoe on a tile. The irregular sputter of a fluorescent bulb. (Galgut 2010, p. 27)

The failed rush for the connecting train can result in 59 minutes of waiting. At the big stations, there are plenty of distractions or places to sit in the dry and warm, or for the sociologist, life to watch. At others, it is an experience of the elements. Quakers talk of 'expectant waiting' as they settle into their still and silent worship. Is an hour's delay a time for prayer or to gather a sense of the spiritual connectedness of all of creation or just time to be filled?

It is not always easy. Sitting at Blackburn station once, I finished the many-times-read supplement picked up on the previous train and waited and watched. Everyone around me was wired in: a nation who knew how to queue publicly has become one used to losing time privately. We create diversion, send a text to get a reply, make endless useless phone calls: 'the train is delayed, I don't know for how long – I'll call you again when I know more'. Can we turn these moments into times or reflection and renewal?

The weather doesn't always help, especially in the north. Bill Bryson wrote this about experience of waiting for a bus.

> There was no bench or shelter by the bus-stop, nowhere to get out of the rain. If you travel much by public transport in Britain these days you soon come to feel like a member of some unwanted sub-class, like the handicapped or unemployed, and that everyone essentially wishes you would just go away. (Bryson 1999, p. 253)

One day, I needed to get to London from Birmingham for a 10am meeting. The return fare was £158 so I went by coach instead for £16! Instead of the 8.20am train, I needed to get the 6am coach. The saving of £142 took an extra six hours out of my day. This meant rising at 4am to get the 4.40am bus from the suburbs of Birmingham. I waited at the bus-stop, cold, hung over with the lack of sleep and in the dark. At last, the birds started singing. The new electronic display told me when the next buses were due, then I saw the distinctive glow of the illuminated sign at the front appearing over the hill in the far distance. It was a ghost bus: there was total eerie silence among the passengers, who read/listened to their devices/slept. All the passengers were men save one. This was the first or second bus of the morning, allowing folk to get to work to allow other folk to get to work, or for those with long commutes: the first bus drivers have to use private transport to get to their work.

The bus windows were all fogged up, but in this state of semi-somnulence, this was a destination-journey, not a process one. Nobody wanted to look out the window anyway. It was like the sleeper train of bus services. Off the bus, there was movement around the market stalls in the middle of Birmingham. The electronic shutters on an arcade went up.

Then I reached the coach station, gleaming and clean and so much better than it used to be. It was a hive of snooze, a den of waiting, of people anxious to get the coach or anxious to get on the coach first so they could get the seat they wanted. Those with longer waits snoozed on. Someone rushed up late for a coach with a ticketing problem – the coach waited, personal contact between passenger and driver allowing patience. The coach finally left five minutes late with two relieved passengers and two virtuous employees seeing it off. It was not a train, not holding anything else up further down the line. My coach came in. It filled. We left. I could not see much, but I could sleep, and it arrived totally on time.

The experience of using buses and coaches is similar to trains, perhaps simply slower and even less comfortable, but cheaper. We are more likely to have a neighbour, find it difficult to have everything we have with us stowed easily. If a week is long time in politics, even a few minutes on a very crowded train or bus can feel eternal. In Kenya, having failed to get on two buses headed for the airport because of the overcrowding, I raced to a third. It was also very full but I got on. I only survived passing out among the extreme throng of passengers by standing on my luggage. I could hardly breathe and yet coming down the bus was the conductor, weaving between passengers through invisible spaces. When I got off, now one of the last people left on the bus, I was still close to fainting and only felt restored about two hours later.

That is an extreme example, but public transport is just that: very public. We can be co-opted into other people's arguments, drawn towards the sharing of food or alcohol, asked questions by complete strangers. At least two prominent politicians have said that the only problem with using public transport is sharing it with other people. At the same time, we can help each other in medical emergencies, build community at the drop of a hat faced with extreme delay or crisis.

Michel de Certeau, in his *The Practice of Everyday Life*, sums up the ambivalence we may feel about travelling by train. He calls it a 'travelling incarceration'; but also a Robinson Crusoe adventure:

A travelling Incarceration. Immobile inside the train, seeing immobile things slip by. What is happening? Nothing is moving inside or outside the train. The unchanging traveller is pigeonholed, numbered, and regulated in the grid of the railway car . . . Control and food move from pigeonhole to pigeonhole: 'Tickets, please . . .' 'Sandwiches? Beer? Coffee . . .' Only the restrooms offer an escape from the closed system. They are a lovers' phantasm, a way out for the ill, an escapade for children ('Wee-wee!') – a little space of irrationality . . . Outside, the scenery is immobile, detached, passing, silent from within the carriage. Coming and going, unbidden and without negotiation, subject to our flickering vision. The window acts as a trader in symmetry between the immobile, part of the rolling partition . . . And, also as always, one has to get out: there are only lost paradises. Is the terminal the end of an illusion? There is another threshold, composed of momentary bewilderments in the airlock constituted by the train station . . . In the mobile world of the train station, the immobile machine suddenly seems monumental and almost incongruous in its mute, idol-like inertia, a sort of god undone. Everyone goes back to work at the place he has been given, in the office or in the workshop. The incarceration-vacation is over. For the beautiful abstraction of the prison are substituted the compromises, opacities and dependencies of the workplace. Hand-to-hand combat begins again with a reality that dislodges the spectator without rails or windowpanes. There comes to an end the Robinson Crusoe adventure of the travelling noble soul that could believe itself *intact* because it was surrounded by glass and iron. (de Certeau 1984, pp. 111, 114)

46

We are moved, and in de Certeau's terms, imprisoned and yet the very prison gives us the freedom to be disembedded from our daily concerns and to feel separated and untouched by all we watch. We have to relinquish that sense of invincibility once we disembark. Of course, today, mobile phones may mean we are never really removed. Indeed, as I show in the next chapter, sometimes we even need to protect ourselves from the intruding lives of others.

Trains may now seem anachronistic in a time when we want to control our travel, but they still allow us to buy into a great variety of travel options, including international ones. Trains can still, at times, not be beaten. The uncrowded train, a window seat at an empty table, with true peace and quiet and good food smoothly speeding through beautiful landscape on an epic journey for hours and hours, is a special treat for me. The ability to sleep, read, watch, all with a constantly changing vista, is pretty perfect.

They can be fast, clean, comfortable, relaxing and spacious if we choose our routes carefully. But sadly, they are also prone to delay and cancellation, appear expensive, are unpredictable in terms of how full they are and how many carriages there may be. Train journeys may feed us spiritually or take huge amounts of emotional labour and leave us frustrated and fraught.

Planes

Flying has become relatively common. Most people in Britain have been on a plane and some use one every week. For foreign travel, going by air is not only the means to an end, but an expectation, born initially out of possibility. As with the increase in commuting when new roads are built, or the expectation that comes out of the possibility of e-mail or mobile phones, 'can' is replaced by 'should'. An increase in disposable income means an increase in the purchase of disposable leisure.

Buying travel is socially acceptable. We buy experience, rest, escape, and while it isn't landfill, the environmental cost of flying to purchase a rest, a tan and some photos to prove we were there, is huge. In actual fact, flying becomes less essential as other technology (e-mail, video-conferencing) takes over. But in terms of leisure, it is now normative for family holidays, even weekends away. Air travel from Britain, even with its comprehensive ground transport systems and options, outstrips the carbon footprint of the USA, where flying is often the only way to travel between cities. The difference is in the costs. Budget airlines, operating out of Britain, have increased the British air travel market hugely. Because we can, we do.

We calculate the lines of most enjoyment through our flying experience: the best places to eat or the cheapest, the best way to carry or wheel our luggage, the time to leave, the time to arrive to check in, the places to stay, what to take and what to leave behind, and where indeed we want to go in the first place and how best to get there. Package trips still take away many of the obsessive's choices, or we can concoct our own itineraries and become our own travel agents thanks to the web.

We may have booked our tickets and secured our choice of seat and meal type months before, but our experience of flying usually starts at least 24 hours before, with the option of an online check-in. We pack. We need to choose what to take and how best to take it. Weight restrictions and the desire to balance our comfort in handling our own luggage and our comfort when we are 'there' can lead to fraught calculations and choices. Cases with wheels allow us to take more with us to reassemble more of home when we are 'away'.

I used to travel with hand luggage only. I never needed to check in a bag and, although going through security could make travel feel more like its etymological root, 'travail' (work!), I was always first out through customs at my destination, not needing to wait for the carousel to start up and finally present my bag to me. More recently I have taken no hand luggage at all. Security has been easier, and I have not had to haul my belongings around the departure lounge. Travelling to America, for example, always involves long waits at 'homeland security' (passport control), and there is then hardly any delay in collecting my luggage. It also means, following 9/11 restrictions, that I can transport marmalade or other gels over 100ml. Within the USA, 'checking' baggage usually costs money, so then I revert to using the bag as hand luggage. Thus, I need a bag that can still count as hand baggage. And so on and so on, we calculate and become practised at negotiating the air transport systems.

We become familiar with certain airports and find the best airports for easy transfers between flights. As we are dripped rewards through air miles, we may start to only travel with certain networks of airlines. We cut down the overwhelming choice of options facing the air traveller. As Sheena Iyengar's research shows, I, like all other consumers, construct arbitrary criteria to help reduce the degree of choice so as to avoid being overwhelmed. Iyengar was the academic who conducted the famous jam study. At the front of a famous delicatessen in California, she was allowed to set up a tasting area of 24 different jams. Lots of people tried the jams but few went on to buy any of them. When the number of tasting options was reduced to six, fewer people stopped to taste, but many more people bought a jar of one of them (Iyengar 2010). When the choice is between more than seven options, we become overwhelmed and so choose arbitrary ways of reducing the field. Buying a car, we may determine it has to be a particular make or have particular options or be a particular colour or be within a ten mile radius so as to allow us to choose more clearly. I have been to Portland, Oregon annually for about 15 years now. For the first ten, I always stayed at the same hotel. One visit, it was already full when I went to book a room and was then told I had the choice of 144 hotels within a square mile of my destination. Overwhelmed, I found and now use a discount website that offers you five choices and only reveals the name of the hotel after you've booked the stay. I was so pleased to have less choice. Airlines may thank us for our loyalty and give us air miles but we also benefit from sticking with a brand.

We choose how to get to the airport. Train or bus or car. Private or taxi or 'airport transfer'. All choices. Getting to the airport on time is crucial. We don't want to miss our flight. Unlike trains, we may not be left stranded for an hour but maybe a day. We may lose our right to fly at all. And, as with much of our travel now, one part of the journey is simply a scheduled prelude to another. We need to make our connection or our meeting. I cycled for months without a watch and sometimes did not even know what day it was. In Jordan once, my companion and I rose at dawn so we could get to Petra before the noon-day sun. After two hours of cycling, it was still not fully light. Tired, we stopped and slept another few hours. Then dawn came! We had originally risen probably at about midnight, but neither of us had any means of telling the time. Last year, I had to get up at 3.30am after two hours' sleep to catch a 6am flight in Wichita. I set three alarms clocks. In this way, we become wedded to the need to know the time and to manage our use of it. Thus, we all find our best ways to travel by air. We choose luggage and airports and airlines. We set clocks. We get to the airport on time if we can.

We have the visas we need and keep our passports up to date. Only in the First World War did passports become a common system of control, and indeed they were only standardized in 1980. Now, they are everything: our proof of identity; our way into and way out of somewhere; our recourse to safety in time of crisis. Our citizenship means we can and will be helped by our embassies wherever we are. Judith Adler emphasizes this 'distribution of risk':

The passport, which signifies that a traveler is backed by the protection of a powerful state ready to intervene on his behalf or repatriate him if necessary, is often his most valuable, indeed his only truly necessary, property. Guaranteeing immunity from travel hazards faced by relatively propertyless people, that is, those protected only by weak states or by none at all, a passport may literally save a traveler's life. Thus, risk is differentially distributed along national lines for otherwise identical travel performances. (Adler 1989, p. 1381)

Visas in contrast are a privilege given us by the country we wish to visit, not a right. Being a citizen of the mother country of an empire has huge benefits; there are still so many places where Britons do not need visas. Passport and tickets are kept safe. Perhaps we have particular clothes for travelling. A coat or jacket with perfect ticket-shaped pockets for safe keeping: I always fly wearing a shirt with a top pocket for this very reason.

We are handled and examined by 'Security'. If we are unlucky, we will have our bag opened and unpacked, as happens to Professor Morris Zapp in David Lodge's novel, *Small World*:

He joins a long line of people shuffling through a security checkpoint. His handbaggage is opened and searched . . . the lady making the search opens a cardboard box, and small, hard cylindrical objects, wrapped in silverfoil, roll into the palm of her hand. '*Bullets*' her eyes seem to enquire. 'Suppositories' Morris Zapp volunteers. Few privacies are vouchsafed to the modern traveller. Strangers rifling through your luggage can tell at a glance the state of your digestive system, what method of contraception you favour, whether you have a denture that requires a fixative, whether you suffer from haemorrhoids, corns, headaches, eye fatigue, flatulence, dry lips, allergic phinitis and premenstrual tension. (Lodge 1984, p. 102)

Then we are free to wait for our flight, for the next movement towards eventual take-off. We can relax after all the procedures have been completed, at least for the time we have before we are called to our 'gate'. We may find the departure lounge settings exciting for all that they connote, and meals there, 'eating out', may symbolize the start of a holiday. However, for me, very busy airports still ooze the anxiety of the unpractised traveller, as I find myself surrounded by too many public crises and arguments. They also feel unreal, closed in and constructed, artificial spaces that separate incoming from outgoing passengers and divide the outgoing into pre- and post-processed. Prolonged interaction highlights this façade. I once waited overnight in Stansted airport, sleeping on the floor. The lights went off, and there seemed to be just myself and my fellow sleepers. At 6am, the lights came on, and the shops opened, and it was if I was in a scene from the film *The Truman Show* (1998). This is a film about a huge reality show, where only one character does not know he is being filmed. Everyone else is an actor, and a TV producer determines when the sun will rise (a switch is flicked) and what will happen that day. The lights came on at Stansted, and it was if everyone had been awake for ages, but for me. At Chicago more recently, after another night on the floor, the airport came awake at 5am.

Every terminal is a hot space, every person creating hot space, moving around in random cycles through shops etc., while we 'kill time'. In other words, the space is anybody's and everybody's. Only the building and the shops remain fixed as millions of people circulate in, through and out of these air-conditioned anywheres. We share it for a time. It is a time we have to spend there, and it is made easier by the distraction of shops or the escape of books or internet. Airports are hybrid spaces of conveying travellers, selling food and other goods to them and maintaining security. We are sold to, and surveilled. They are in some ways subject to what sociologist Alan Bryman has called 'Disneyization' (1999). He suggests Disneyization is centred on four concepts: theming; the de-differentiation of consumption; merchandizing; and emotional labour (p. 29). Airports (and motorway service stations) become shopping centres and a whole lot else as 'conventional distinctions between casinos, hotels, restaurants, shopping, and theme parks collapse' (p. 36). Everything is merchandized. Airports are no one thing. In Manchester Airport's Terminal Two, the path to the departure gates winds its way through a duty-free sales outlet. We are on the way to our plane but in a shop. We are suddenly turned into potential customers within a shop we didn't even ask to enter. While we 'kill time' in the departure lounge, shops and bars and cafes and gaming machines try to encourage us to think of our money as equally disposable.

The airport prayer room offers us a non-commercial space apart to gather ourselves before and after, a recognition of faith adherence but also a symbol of a secular society in that we are to pray apart and hidden. We can of course be still and quiet and offer our prayers for those around us anywhere: the anxious flyer, the person missing their connection, or missing their partner, those in tears awaiting a relative. Indeed, we may be better off trying to practise our faith in public: the airport prayer rooms I have visited are empty sterile spaces, open to all traditions and enriched by none.

Airports are not all exactly alike of course, hence our choice of the best ones to travel through. We may prefer those with free wireless or less distance to walk. We may prefer less busy ones or newer ones. At Manchester, I found there was no free water, for example, a desiccated contrast to all the water fountains in airports in the USA.

We may catch a bus to the plane or use a 'walkway', an extending carpeted bridge that sits somewhere between the definition of inside and outside. It is inside because it is covered but rain coming in at the edges as it pushes away further from the main terminal suggests it is not fully within, a further example of hybridization. Then we are ready to board the flying machine.

As we enter the bigger jets, the rich or privileged 'go left', the rest go right. Paying more buys space, privacy and service. First-class airline seats turn into semi-private bed 'rooms'. On the smaller planes, we as 'everyperson' wander past the big plush seats of business class, staring to see what we're missing out on (the stare as one perk of not being there for longer). Then the curtain is pulled across between the seating areas to complete the class divide.

We may not of course fly directly to where we want to go. To cut costs, airlines use 'hubs'; and we fly there and change planes, prolonging travel times and increasing pollution. But we are on the move. We can now relax more fully. We have made the flight and all being well it will take off on time. We have our own seat and, with no immediate responsibilities, can create a temporary home or workplace. Along the way, we are offered as compensation for the time the journey takes and the physical discomfort, the technological means, via film or power socket, to escape even our travel. Even if we have visited a website showing how much extra leg room this particular airline gives us, only a few of us have access to a window. Most of us have to be content with personal music players, books, sleep, or the all-pervasive screens. Where there are communal screens, we struggle to see, watching a film in an airborne cinema that we didn't ask to visit. With a personal screen, we can now watch a choice of films, stop, pause, rewind or play computer games. We are given the means to avoid the experience of travel. And as the technology gets more sophisticated, we are charged additionally for its use. Now we take 'watching' for granted as the dominant experience of flight, we will pay for headphones or the new 'entertainment options'. We may buy our own 'noise cancelling headphones' to maximize the ability to not be present to all around us.

Feeding times also lend distraction. Free food, even in its packaged form in a cramped seat and with plastic cutlery, is a perk, abandoned by budget airlines and no longer available on domestic flights. In *Small World*, academic Persse McGarrigle flies from London to Los Angeles.

It is dark by the time they begin their descent to Los Angeles, and the city is an awe-inspiring sight from the air – a glimmering gridiron of light from horizon to horizon – but Persse, who has been travelling for twenty-two hours, is too tired to appreciate it. He has tried to sleep on two planes, but they kept waking him up to give him meals. Long-distance flying, he decides, is rather like being in hospital in that respect, and it wouldn't have surprised him unduly if one of the hostesses had slipped a thermometer in his mouth between meals. He had scarcely the strength to rip open the plastic envelope containing his cutlery for the last dinner he was offered. (Lodge 1984, p. 272)

Mostly, long-distance flying is exhausting. We get up early or get to sleep late, change time zones and confuse our bodies. We travel all too quickly and all too slowly. All too quickly because time is lost, covered over, recalibrated: we arrive in a new time zone, adjust our watches, 'dust ourselves down and start all over again'. All too slowly, because of the very sense of needing to fill travel in with music and messages and movies.

Jet lag becomes an area we also need to strategize around. Do we stay awake, take a short nap, sleep on the plane if we can? Do we not eat on the plane and trick our bodies by eating the first major meal in the next destination as one study suggests? (Fuller et al. 2008). At the other end of the long-distance overnight flight, we emerge as shell-shocked red-eye arrivals to be further bewildered by the sea of faces of those waiting to meet someone. Maybe we are meeting friends and family we haven't seen for decades, and consolation for the journey is immediate. Maybe we are met by a dour chauffeur half-heartedly holding a sign with our name on it. Maybe we are coming home, back from elsewhere. Often we come back from holiday in the clothing we wore when we were away. Maybe that was the most practical thing to do. Maybe we are eager to show off our newly created tans, in denial about how really cold and miserable Britain can be, or maybe we are just trying to hold on to our experience of being somewhere else, away from the daily routines, for a few hours longer.

Flying is not always a situation of ordeal. I have enjoyed so many flights. I build a home by the window and love looking out at all that we pass by. I have seen amazing mountains and deserts and cityscapes and storms. I have been frightened and exhilarated. I have had flights with plenty of space, both in front of me and beside me, and lovely food. I have flown without queuing and without rushing for connections. Mainly, however, it is an experience of being herded and regulated. I suggest that airports are sites of potential trauma, filled with anxiety/fear/inspection/goodbyes/hallos/and above all, regulation. We hand our lives over to be managed in terms of task (the promise to fulfil our need to get 'there') and by technology. We contract in to formality, regulation and distraction, and we are sold gear to make the endurance easier. All the strategies that the seasoned traveller adopts: priority booking; travelling only with hand luggage or with no hand luggage at all – all the preferred routines, only give so much pleasure to their inventors because of the adversity they are designed to overcome. Flying is not pleasurable, and for many, not even romantic any more or pioneering. It is no longer exotic. Like all new technologies, the excitement of 'the new', of all that can now be unusually attained, becomes routine and an expectation. Benefits, like the 24-hour access of mobile phones, become a cost (like never being away from the office). As one Air Jamaica steward told me, 'Other than my work, I never fly anywhere now, it is too much hassle.' Air travel is rarely about the journey, but the arriving and resting after its ardours: 'getting there' is no longer 'half the fun'.

Automobiles

Motor cars appear to offer a way of travel that gets around many of the unappealing aspects of train and plane travel. Cars cannot cross oceans of course but for most of us they are our main means of travel. We can choose when to go and whom to travel with. In other words, we are not squeezed into somebody else's timetable or into somebody else's space, squeezed up next to somebody we don't really want to sit beside. We can choose our route, our speed, whether or not to be in silence or listening to music. We can smoke. We can travel door to door when we wish. We can go places we wouldn't otherwise go or couldn't otherwise get to on public transport. We can carry more than we could by train and resurrect more of 'home' than we ever used to be able to, when say camping. We can be in control of our travel.

I find many cars very beautiful, externally and internally. They are also a critical part of our social history over the last decade. The popularity of the car has meant that it has become a dominant consideration in business and town planning. To ease parking problems and to take advantage of cheap land, new shopping centres have been built away from the centre of towns based on the assumption of car ownership. Thus, the whole way we shop and the whole look of town centres has been dominated by the popularity of the car. As Matthew Paterson suggests: 'Cars are globally the predominant daily form of mobility. Even for those who do not use a car, the conditions under which we move around are shaped fundamentally by car-led development strategies' (2007, p. 9).

Cars make life easier. Added concerns about the safety of children walking to school have been eased for some by the possibility of driving them there. Now the 'school run' extends the 'rush hour'. As is happening with mobile telephones, what starts as a convenient option comes to be seen as a necessity. Those without appear to be deviant.

Cars symbolize and offer freedom and, like bicycles before them, have allowed a nation to become mobile. Unlike with bicycles, with cars we can cover huge distances in a day while doing very little ourselves. They epitomize 'the good life'. Toad in *The Wind in the Willows* needed only a short encounter to move his allegiances from his beloved painted carts to the motor car.

> 'There you are!' cried the Toad, straddling and expanding himself. 'There's real life for you, embodied in that little cart. The open road, the dusty highway, the heath, the common, the hedgerows, the rolling downs! Camps, villages, towns, cities! Here to-day, up and off to somewhere else to-morrow! Travel, change, interest, excitement! The whole world before you, and a horizon that's always changing! (Grahame 1995, p. 51)

Moments later, nearly run down by a car, he had changed his mind:

> 'Glorious, stirring sight!' murmured Toad . . . 'The poetry of motion! The *real* way to travel! The *only* way to travel! Here to-day – in next week to-morrow! Villages skipped, towns and cities jumped – always somebody else's horizon! O bliss! O poop-poop! O my! O my!' . . . 'And to think I

never *knew*!' went on the Toad in a dreamy monotone. 'All
those wasted years that lie behind me, I never knew, never
even *dreamt*! But *now* – but now that I know, now that I
fully realise! O what a flowery track lies spread before me,
henceforth! What dust-clouds shall spring up behind me as
I speed on my reckless way! What carts I shall fling care-
lessly into the ditch in the wake of my magnificent onset!
Horrid little carts – common carts – canary-coloured carts!'
(Grahame 1995, pp. 35, 45)

Some opulent models are lush to sit in, truly living rooms on
wheels. Motoring writer L. J. K. Setright went so far as to
suggest that the central heating of cars led to the mass central heating of homes (2004, p. 351). Once we added a windscreen to the horseless carriage, the logic of full bodywork
and heating followed.

We so like cars, or feel we need one so much, that we are
prepared to take out loans second only to mortgages in size
to buy them (Urry 2011, p. 121). Given their cost, they can
symbolize status and achievement. Manufacturers play on this
allure to sell us their latest models. We stop and stare at the
exotic car. Some people's lifetime ambitions are based on the
ownership of a particular model. Like jam or airlines, we have
all constructed our own preferred marques as best, and make
choices based on emotional 'logic'.

Equally, we spend more money than we might need to on
cars because we are frightened of their unreliability. While we
take religious authority more and more into our own hands, we
still rely on highly priced experts to diagnose and fix our automobiles. The unwitting can be taken for a metaphorical ride.

We are also aware of their dangers and strap ourselves in for
safety. Sociologists like John Urry have argued that the term
'motor accident' is a misnomer as risk seems built into this
form of travel (2011, p. 118). Cars now come with multiple

airbags and increasingly isolate us from the outside. Emergency vehicles have needed new types of sirens to overcome the insulation brought on by the prevalence of air conditioning and high fidelity within cars. We can feel invincible in our cars and dodge traffic as if we are in a computer game. Other cars do not contain people, just other drivers also playing the game that we need to win.

This dehumanization of other road users is not true everywhere. Shreve Stockton talks of the human connection being honoured 'even on the road' among her neighbours in rural Wyoming:

> Cars are not barriers or personal bubbles as they are in the city. Drivers make eye contact when they pass one another and nearly everyone waves, stranger or not. Even in separate vehicles, there is an intimacy; it is an acknowledgement of another human in this vast scape, and of treating them as a comrade. (Stockton 2008, p. 9)

The contrast Stockton makes with the city, however, underlines the general idea that cars separate us: they give us the private means to go where we want to, and their very isolation is part of their attraction. The way classic car owners wave at each other, or the way we wave at passing trains, steam trains in particular, signals excitement at seeing such a machine but also a connection between us as travellers who know what it used to be like to travel. The wave, I suggest, affirms the journey-maker as someone setting off with intention and moment. It harkens back to a day when all journeys needed to be intentional and thought through. It is a wave of nostalgia in remembrance of slower and more daring adventures that risked mechanical failure or an ember in the eye.

Cars are loved by many and hated by others. Subject to tirades from environmentalists or militant pedestrians and cyclists, always costly and usually depreciating, sometimes unreliable and yet such a personalized form of private convenience, the car fills an ambiguous place in our affections. Bill Bryson writes of them:

> Motorised vehicles are ugly and dirty and they bring out the worst in people. They clutter every kerbside, turn ancient market squares into disorderly jumbles of metal, spawn petrol stations, second-hand car lots, Kwik-Fit centres and other dispiriting blights. (Bryson 1999, p. 64)

Mostly though, we love them more than we hate them. We assume their use as part of our life and thus feel we 'need them'. Ultimately, cars are popular. However, it is this very popularity which seems to undermine the joys of driving. In other words, there are so many cars on the British roads that driving is less of an unalloyed joy than it once may have been. We experience traffic jams, delays and cannot be sure of when we will arrive. John Urry comments: 'People inhabit congestion, jams, temporal uncertainties and health-threatening city environments through being encapsulated in a domestic, cocooned, moving capsule, an iron bubble' (2011, p. 120).

Today, we travel more easily and more automatically. Both aspects of auto-mobility have led to several factors that make it potentially more stressful. Traffic is denser and more quickly moving than before and we risk censure if we drive too slowly. Other drivers scare us with their driving or threaten us, and we now need to manage the possibility of 'road rage'.

At the same time, running a car, while a modern expectation, is not straightforward. The cost of fuel has made many of us use our cars less or combine trips or we watch anxiously as the needle on the fuel gauge drops. Large cars become even more ambivalent symbols to aspire towards while retaining their status identity even because of the cost of running them. In the meantime, the smaller models get bigger and a new status race has developed around fuel consumption rather than acceleration and speed. Driving is fraught with potential stresses and strains.

We drive as close to our destinations as we can because car travel is enshrined within a logic of convenience. Circling huge shopping centre car parks to try and get a parking space closer to the store seems to defeat the object sometimes, but the whole point of car travel is door-to-door convenience. The impulse of car use means we even drive to the gym! We are suffering from travel sickness too in terms of the sedentary nature of much of how we are moved; as levels of obesity rise, we do not exercise more, simply get bigger cars and use them more.

Car parks are overcrowded and offer too little space per car. Doors touch the other car and tempers can ignite. Car parking space is a new commodity and the demand for it has changed the face of many of our cities. These car parks can also be costly so we need to strategize about where to park and when to travel.

Cars have become unreliable in this way as means of convenience. We have to leave early or 'allow extra time'. We drive faster to make up time or find we can only enjoy the speed of a car for shorter periods of time. Friends travelling from Carlisle to Cornwall for holidays used to leave at midnight to be sure of their travel time. In this sense, cars can become outmoded as the preferred means of long-distance travel. The timing of their optimal use becomes inconvenient rather than convenient.

While we can see drivers dwarfed by the size of their vehicles, many popular cars, when filled with people, offer only cramped conditions with little extra space for luggage. In the ways cars are currently designed, the rear passengers have a limited forward view. The seating arrangements do not suit conversation.

We may be tempted to take the train. Compared with a coach using the bus lane, filled with 50 people, a long line of cars waiting to enter our big cities every morning appears as an exercise in foolery.

As with planes, we have adapted our vehicles to become more comfortable for waiting and delay as well as movement and travel. Cars can become our temporary or second homes or mobile offices, highly personalized and highly personal. We are surrounded by the means of relaxation to offset the stress of much driving. They can become our own created worlds, air conditioned with the music of our choice, now even with DVD players and sockets for phones, cup holders and GPS navigation systems. It is our space, not a place to look out from but one to enjoy until arrival. 'The ubiquitousness of the radio and to some extent of air conditioning . . . insulates the passengers from almost all aspects of the environment except the view through the windscreen' (Urry 2002, p. 55). Now the advent of in-car DVD systems even makes the passenger window redundant. In modern cars, windows are rarely opened. Passing through is now passing by. Privacy glass hides us from the world we do not want to see or be seen by. Humbert Humbert in *Lolita* says: 'We have been everywhere. We have seen nothing' (Jakle 1985, p. 198).

I have been told that only 37 per cent of drivers claim they enjoy driving but still the other 63 per cent persevere, pushed on to the roads by an illusion, or memory, of control or convenience – we only have ourselves to 'blame' when these personal trains of ours arrive late. We can of course now phone from the car. We use one technology to offset the limits of using another. As with trains and planes, we are left managing adversity.

In Sharon Butala's novel, *Country of the Heart*, the young heroine, Lannie, reflects on why she had chosen not to own a car:

Without a car, she would tell herself, she never had to worry about an oil change, or a funny noise, or a place to park. She was never stranded, as she sometimes would have been with one, when it wouldn't start or had a flat. Without a car she was free. (Butala 1999, p. 3)

Pedestrians and Pedal Cycles

Our use of trains, planes and automobiles all harm the environment but cars also affect the more manual means of motions, walking and cycling. As sociologist Richard Sennett comments:

we take unrestricted motion of the individual to be an absolute right. The private motorcar is the logical instrument for exercising that right, and the effect on public space, especially the space of the urban street, is that the space becomes meaningless or even maddening unless it can be subordinated to free movement. (Sennett 1977, p. 14)

Cars dominates the street. Cars can easily kill a walker or cyclist and we do well to keep out of their way. As pedestrians we have to watch for cars that do not stop at Zebra crossings, that break the speed limits, that mount the kerb to park and who treat the pavements as a continuation of the road or a car park.

Space for pedestrians is continually eroding. In my local supermarkets, it becomes a danger to walk to their doors across areas designed solely for cars. In the suburbs of America, often built without pavements, people become imprisoned without a car. Children in these areas watch four times as much television as those living in less constrained areas (Kay 1998, p. 25).

As cyclists, we need to be sure we are seen. I know cyclists who still refuse to put lights on their bicycles because in the

1920s and 1930s, it was the responsibility of the car driver. Cyclists without helmets or lights are now seen to be the authors of the tragedy when a car hits them. It is interesting that research shows that cars give helmetless cyclists more room (Walker 2007). When we start to make humans look like machines, we care less.

Sundays, once the day for cycling on less busy roads, is now a prime shopping day and there is never a quieter time for bicycling. We are always at equal risk.

There are choices. In Portland, Oregon, cars give way to pedestrians crossing the end of side streets. Different choices have been made and inform the dynamic between walker and driver. Cycle paths abound; cycles can be carried on buses. Many drivers are cyclists and are sympathetic. So much of how we can travel well and share the space is about building empathy. In our mobile 'iron cages' we lose that sense of connection with other travellers, equally locked away, and with those precariously uncaged who walk or cycle.

Our personal experience of travel is not always good in part due to the popularity and commodification of travel. As the market has increased, so train and plane carriers have tried to get more people into fewer machines. As drivers, we are part of the dis-ease of motoring popularity, increasingly stressed because so many other people have made the same transport choice as us. In the next chapter, I look at how our forms of travel segregate us from each other as travellers and also segregate us from those we travel among.

An Aside on Speed and Time

As mentioned above, speed is often the criterion by which we choose our mode of travel. Walking from Manchester to London would take at least a week, or we can take the train in just over two hours or fly in half of that. The popularization and commodification of travel has been accompanied by the commodification of time.

Everything becomes timetabled. Unstructured time and indeterminate travel becomes a rarity, as Rebecca Solnit argues:

> The multiplication of technologies in the name of efficiency is actually eradicating free time by making it possible to maximize the time and place for production and minimize the unstructured travel time in between . . . The indeterminacy of a ramble, on which much may be discovered, is being replaced by the determinate shortest distance to be traversed with all possible speed, as well as by the electronic transmissions that make real travel less necessary. (Solnit 2002, p. 10)

Tobias Jones shows how private transport allows us to make our own plans and schedules, often stretching possibility into endurance:

> I drive thousands of miles every year to see friends and relatives who live on the other side of the country or the continent. None of us live in the same neighbourhood anymore and mobility is the neurotic result. We're never at home for the weekend. I seem to be suffering from an inability to stop and belong. Where I stand used to be the centre of my world, but it's no longer like that. The world has shrunk exponentially and now, instead of feeling at home where I actually am, I imagine home is wherever I'm not . . . We've all become consumers of distance, breaking down boundaries as we career from one destination to the next. We're perpetually ahead of ourselves, trying to get somewhere else before everyone else. It's a truism of our way of life that we're constantly in-touch but out-of-place . . . Speed becomes paramount. Computer connection or five

gear estate, I've got to get there quickly. If I ever get caught in traffic, or in a shop queue, I'm insufferable, impatient, moody: 'Get out of my way' I whisper through gritted teeth. I'm addicted to a way of life. Like all addictions, it gets worse the longer it goes on. The joys are more intermittent, the sorrow always increasing. I'm spending far too much money and working harder to earn more so that I can travel further and faster and screw the neighbours. (Jones 2007, p. 9–10)

As we travel greater distances, speed becomes more important. We don't travel for longer necessarily, we just travel further at greater speed.

This chapter has said little about spirituality, it has been more about exploring how we travel using systems that allow us to travel with less sense of risk. But I do believe that we should be wary of the speed at which we seek to cover distance, to complete the travel-task. I am sure that 'keeping the pace' is as important as 'keeping the peace' in our spiritual journeys. John Woolman, eighteenth-century Quaker, had a similar concern. He counselled that we should 'keep pace with the gentle motions of Truth' (Moulton 1971, p. 70). In other words, let us not outrun our guide, or, to quote the bumper sticker, 'Never travel faster than our angel can fly'! If we are discerning our travel, we need to discern both the 'what' and the 'when'. It is true of discerning anything. Timing is as important as content. We need to be clear about what it is we are called to do and when it is we are called to enact that leading.

If we fall short, we may feel spiritually adrift. In the world of mobility, 'speed kills'. John Woolman eventually refused to use the stagecoach system, what he called the 'flying coach' (1925, p. 18), when he visited England in 1772 because of the effects it had on the horses and the postboys who rode them and those knocked down by the coaches at night:

Stagecoaches frequently go upwards of a hundred miles in 24 hours, and I have heard Friends say in several places that it is common for horses to be killed with hard driving, and many others driven till they grow blind. These coaches running chief part of the night do often run over foot people in the dark . . . Postboys pursue their business, each one to his stage, all night through the winter. Some boys who ride long stages suffer greatly in winter nights, and at several places I have heard of their being froze to death. So great is the hurry in the spirit of this world that in aiming to do business quick and to gain wealth the creation at this day doth loudly groan! (Moulton 1971, p. 183)

With our cars, we simply add better seat belts or air bags to protect the occupants more. We have bonnets that will crumple under the weight of the pedestrian hit by a car. In short, we use technology to offset the dangers of speed rather than limiting speed in the first place. Now we are seeing 20mph zones in town centres to prevent fatalities, but in the same way we inveigh against speed cameras this is felt by some as a betrayal of the freedom of the car-driver.

When I have driven along the motorway at 50mph (improving our fuel consumption by about 10 per cent), I have been treated as an inconvenience, in spite of the two passing lanes to the right. Only a sticker untruthfully saying that the vehicle was speed-limited reduced the angst of those eager to get past and get on. How fast would we all go if we didn't have a speed limit? Why is speed more important than our carbon footprint?

Has the 'rinse cycle' of the train journey gone into a turbo spin? Are fast journeys as restful as slower ones? Is part of the British love affair with preserving steam trains (Carter 2012, p. 57) partly connected with the yearning for a slower pace of travel?

I put in a plea for the pace of travel being part of our discernment. Let us not worry if it makes us unpopular. In the Conclusion to *Walden*, Henry Thoreau writes, 'If a man does not keep pace with his companions, perhaps it is because he hears a different drummer. Let him step to the music which he hears, however measured or far away' (1995, p. 210).

Let us be true to our spiritual insights.

The Unnecessary Obstacles of Travel

The increase in levels of popular travel has made it less special or extra-ordinary. We all travel more and the consequence is that often our travel is less enjoyable. We endure an increasingly dislocating experience of relocating for the sake of reliability. Our experience of travel is more easily facilitated but as it burgeons, is set amid an increased set of compensations whereby cars become lounges, airports one big shop or restaurant and where planes become cinemas. Cruise ships are hotels that happen to float, a travelling 'nowhere' on the nonparticularity of oceans, until they dock. In all these cases, we are encouraged to forget the discomforts of motion or of the means of motion until we arrive.

Sport has been defined by Bernard Suits as 'the voluntary attempt to overcome unnecessary obstacles' (2005). Suits talked about a 'lusory attitude' or the psychological attitude required of a player entering into a game. To adopt a lusory attitude is to accept the arbitrary rules of a game in order to facilitate the experience of play. Thus:

To play a game is to attempt to achieve a specific state of affairs [prelusory goal], using only means permitted by rules [lusory means], where the rules prohibit use of more efficient in favour of less efficient means [constitutive rules], and where the rules are accepted just because they make possible such activity [lusory attitude]. (Suits 2005, pp. 54–5)

I suggest this is a useful way to think about the way we travel now. It has become the voluntary attempt to overcome unnecessary obstacles. Unnecessary, because we could travel differently or far less, points discussed in Chapters 4 and 5. I needed a plumbing part from a shop eight miles away the other Sunday. I had no car, so I rang a friend and borrowed one for an hour. I could have caught the bus, circumventing the stresses of driving, the need to buy fuel, think about insurance and travel anti-socially in a private capsule. On so many counts, this hour did not connect me in a positive way with the rest of creation or enhance my spiritual life. Instead, I opted for convenience and speed. I played the game all drivers play. My goal was to buy and fetch the plumbing part, and I adopted the rules of the road to get it as quickly as possible. I couldn't drive as quickly as I wanted, as I needed to observe speed limits and the courtesies of the road, which allow us all to travel more safely. I 'won' by getting there and back quickly. I 'won' by parking just outside the store as another car left. I 'won' at a number of traffic lights. My journey had become a competition or game, and I lost all sense of the joys of travel or of the process of travel. It was about goal and destination and time.

Even for those of us concerned for our spiritual lives, we are rushing from place to place for work or for leisure, but all too rarely for God. Time and busy-ness have impacted the personal spiritual journey, and we have lost touch with why we go anywhere or what criteria we should use to decide when and when not to go and how to go. We are left with the need to 'manage' the discomforts of travel, so that even these strategies become accepted parts of our social life.

3

Missing the Connection

If the systems of travel we use are stressful, then, I suggest, it has an effect on the way we find ourselves travelling. We may find we need to look after ourselves in among the mass appeal of mass transit by creating our own spaces in which to 'pass the journey'. One of the appeals of cars is that they give us that private space that is so rare when travelling by public means. Travelling today, then, may be most bearable and enjoyable when we are alone or can ignore our fellow travellers, and the first part of this chapter looks at some of the ways we segregate ourselves when on the move. In the second part, I consider how this 'disconnection' plays out when we are visiting somewhere else, as tourists or travellers, and what this sense of separation does to our relationships with those we travel among. I consider the distance we put between ourselves and the rest of humanity, even while we so want to 'see the world' in terms of trying to replicate a sense of 'home' while being away from it. The more ill at ease we feel, the more we may try to establish and impose home comforts and routines in our new settings. Travelling in this way segregates us to the degree we are segregated at home. This strategy of separation from other travellers and those we travel among not only takes us away from the sense of connection we find so clearly at peak moments in our spiritual life but also militates against the attitude of cosmopolitanism or respect for all of humanity, that flows from it. In other words, segregation desacralizes, or secularizes, our travel. It takes us away from being a part of the whole.

Privacy in Public Places

Wolfgang Schivelbusch makes much of how the technology of the railway was so distinct from everyday life in the nineteenth century that railway stations marked a transition point or gateway between the street and the train.

> Thus the station functioned as a gateway which had to connect two very different kinds of traffic and traffic space with another: the traffic space of the city, and that of the railroad. One part of it, the neoclassical stone building, belonged to the city; the other part, the steel and glass construct, was a pure function of the railroad's 'industrial' side. By means of this two-facedness, the railroad station's function as a gateway found its architectural expression. As the departing traveller proceeded from the city, through the reception building, to the train hall, traversing these qualitatively different spaces, he [sic] experienced a process of expansion of space, one might even say, of industrialization of space. Leaving the urban space of the city (in the 1850s, still relatively reassuring), he entered the station's space, which in turn prepared him for the actual industrial space of the railroad. (Schivelbusch 1986, p. 174)

Today, trains may appear to us as just large gadgets in a life filled up with appliances. With the modernization of trains, planes and cars, we are even less connected to their workings. We do not smell coal, see steam, watch out for flying soot, or often gaze at propellers. When something goes wrong with a car, we ask someone with another appliance to plug it into a computer to diagnose the fault. We do not hear engines very much as we travel. Indeed, railway stations are no longer distinct points of transition. Their architecture may not be that unusual and we probably arrive there by means of another engine. Travel in this way blends more effortlessly and seamlessly into our everyday life. The journey becomes the transition, the moment of shifting between worlds.

If we live in a big city, we then start our journey in perhaps no different a mental attitude from the one we walk down the street with. Even in towns we rarely greet or converse with everyone we meet. Rebecca Solnit, in her book on walking, talks of 'the communal solitude of urban walkers' (2002, p. 195). We move from the everyday life of the street to the arena of mass transportation without needing to change how we are with each other. We are practised at mobile solitude. Because 'the journey' is no longer special, we are not waved off by crowds of the well-wishing and curious, and we may not feel our travel is particularly significant. It could be the journey we take every day to work. We may travel in our coats, not relaxing, guarded by buttons and collars. Typically we try and put off anyone sitting next to us, placing our bag on the seat or sitting by the aisle to make it less straightforward for someone to take the seat next to us. We want to enjoy the travel time as much as possible and therefore we may also try and avoid the realities of the journey.

One of the most common ways we avoid our journeys is to secure an auditory eclipse of all that is around us by donning earphones and listening to music. We are taken away into another place and cannot hear the conversations of those around us. Even more consuming is the DVD played on an iPad or netbook: we don't even need to see those around us. Or we may read a book, ideally a good one. As Gwendolen says in Act II of *The Importance of Being Earnest*: 'I never travel without my diary. One should always have something sensational to read in the train' (Wilde 2003, p. 65). We can now 'surf the web' or text on the move. Daily life is not left totally behind any more but travelling becomes an extension of the social relations we are travelling away from or towards. We may be starting or finishing off work, texting a thank-you for the hospitality just received or letting a loved one know when we will arrive. Our journeys are no longer only journeys, they are Disneyized (Bryman 1999). In other words, they may have the theme of 'journey' but are no longer just one thing. They are a work-journey or a text-journey or a film-journey or a web-journey and often a mix of many of these. I usually read on the 'milk train', then do my main work on the intercity.

Another strategy of disengagement with our neighbours is to take over the space as if no one else is there. Perhaps we talk loudly on our phones, spread out uncaringly. We co-opt the space as our own. Mobile phones allow us not only contact on the move but moving contact. Now, freed of a cord, we can physically express our feelings as we talk, pacing up and down for purposeful business calls or swirl and whirl around in the eddies and currents of an intimate exchange. We can 'display-phone'. Maybe those of us with mobile phones speak loudly into them to share some of that joy or urgency, especially when constrained by a railway seat and therefore unable to freely pace or twist. Alternatively, we can be so lost in personal worlds of rhythm, that we sing along out loud (to ourselves) or drum the rhythm on the table; 'private' pleasures invade the public arena.

Few of us regularly engage with the stranger neighbours we find seated next to us. Sat side by side without eye contact with only the journey in common, why should we 'interrupt' the space of another and start a conversation? In Britain, or rather in England, which has a high population density, we are experts at co-habiting tight spaces without intruding. We even apologize when someone else bumps into us. It normally takes a break in the regularized systematization of travel to get us talking: a delay, passing a cup of tea across to the window seat, letting someone in or out. Even then, the conversation may be short-lived, temporary in the way that we assume the companionship will be. And, if we do not talk to each other much, why not don earphones instead of tuning into the 'silent discourse' around us? If we travel first class, we are given enough space to avoid talking to anyone else altogether, a perfect solution for the rich introvert. We create our location to escape time and context.

It might sound like a good opportunity for prayer, but generally we gather ourselves up in a tethered or distracted silence. We are rarely 'beyond ourselves', 'out of time' in a spiritual sense, cast deep into holy no-time, in that enthralling spiral towards God. We are just trying to pass the time.

A friend of mine was on a train leaving Budapest for Germany. The scenery was apparently wonderful, and he was revelling in the journey and all that was before and around him. At the table opposite a group of four placed their iPad up against the window and shared pictures of their holiday to Peru. Maybe they were local and made this journey every day, maybe Peruvian land-scapes trumped Hungarian ones for them. Maybe we are just so used to not living in the present that we reach a state where we are always somewhere else. Do we want to travel at all or just be at our destination? Are we so short of time now given all the demands of modern life that we cannot afford to enjoy the journey and look out of the window or talk to a stranger?

In Savannah, Georgia, in 2006, I was on an early morning flight to Philadelphia. It was small plane, maybe three seats across, two on one side of the aisle, one on the other. I had a neighbour, and we greeted each other, but little more was to be said, and he closed his eyes and tried to retrieve some of the night he had lost through such an early start. When smoke started to come into the cabin as we took off though, he opened his eyes, and we did exchange some reassuring banter. The air steward had already demonstrated her direct manner in the pre-flight safety instructions which had included the phrase, 'if you come past this line, I'll take you down'. Now she stood up again and said, passing out wet towels to those beginning to cough, 'There is no need to panic. You panic when I panic.' A minute later: 'There is no need to worry, the pilot is fully aware of the situation. There is smoke in the cockpit too.' This was not exactly comforting! We were told we were turning back and would undertake an emergency landing. When on another occasion, I had to turn back to an airport, they had used up fuel first but not this time. We were going straight back. The coughing had grown louder. We were told that we were to evacuate the plane as soon as we landed and leave all luggage on board. 'But my computer is in there, it's my whole life', my neighbour exclaimed. 'I bet you have everything backed up . . . (he nodded) . . . I have a book manuscript with 40 hours of editing written on to it and no copy', I responded. 'Oh.' As we came to land, the fire trucks wailed along us, lights flashing. Savannah is a small airport, and I suggested that the emergency services had probably been waiting years for such a moment. We taxied to the edge of the airport field and followed the instructions of the steward and ended up standing on the grass, the coldest in silver blankets. Firefighters in big spacesuits then stormed the plane with hoses while my neighbour and myself (I never did learn his name) looked on plaintively wondering if we would ever see our luggage, or see it dry, again. Six hours later, we were allowed on to the plane to retrieve 'the whole of his life' and my marked-up text. All was well. In the meantime, we spoke easily, but as we went to respective alternative flights, the pragmatic friendship was over.

What would it be like to really be present to the journey? To be aware of the miles travelled, the world outside we pass across, the community inside the vehicle? How different that might be. Lone travellers may be annoyed or disturbed by a group of high-spirited travellers, friends returning from a day in the capital full of the awe and wonder at whatever they have seen, or full of a day at the away-game. They may be rowdy, noisy, boisterous but they are at least talking with each other. They are connecting. We may be fearful if they have been drinking alcohol or fearful of not getting our work done on time, or just fearful of what engagement may cost us. I even got off a train at the wrong station once because I was being drawn by some drinking football fans into a conversation about pubs in my town and football and was so uncomfortable, I needed to escape. I projected my own sense of my privileged background and social separation on to how I thought they would see me/judge me. I see now that they were simply thinking of me as 'one of the lads' and it was I who couldn't get to that point of treating everyone the same. Their behaviour was more cosmopolitan than mine.

In our own cars, we select our company. We play music or audio books, talk on the telephone. We may have given up map reading and use a satellite navigation system. We are plugged in to devices, to other spaces, to help us manage the journey emotionally or literally. The satellite navigation system tells us where to go. We need no local or regional knowledge any more, do not need to know the names of places or the distances between them. We are taken from A to B and B to C without ever needing to understand the lie of the land we are travelling through or even how close C is to A. Even though they are notoriously troublesome, directing people to drive into lakes and taking juggernauts down impossibly impassable lanes, these devices are now more popular than maps. We don't need to stop to check directions either. We are tracked by the satellite and only need to put in our destination to be given directions. We simply drive and listen. We are like a figure in a video game played by satellite. Cars and their technology separate us from the world we pass through.

In an air-conditioned four-wheel-drive Toyota Land Cruiser – the medium through which senior diplomats and top Western relief officials often encounter Africa – suspended high above the road and looking out through closed windows, your fore-head and underarms comfortably dry, you may learn some-thing about Africa. Traveling in a crowded public bus, flesh pressed upon wet, sour flesh, you learn more; and in a 'bush taxi' or 'mammy wagon' where there are not even windows, you learn even more still. But it is on foot that you learn the most. You are on the ground, at the same level with Africans rather than looking down at them. You are no longer pro-tected by speed or air-conditioning or thick glass. The sweat pours from you, and your shirt sticks to your body. This is how you learn. (Kaplan 1996, p. 25)

We separate and we are separated in our desire to make travel as comfortable as possible. When we arrive, this tendency to isolation continues.

Them and Us

I suggest that the way we travel, particularly on shorter jour-neys, mirrors the way we manage our social relations at home. If we live in a highly segregated way, we will organize our travel to replicate that isolation elsewhere. The private jets of the very wealthy give an extreme example of the isolation money can bring. It is convenient but also separate. Another way of looking at this relationship between the way we travel and the way we are in the everyday is that we try to replicate our sense of home, or what home represents, as far as possible wherever we are. We carry with us not only the totems of home life but also the social dynamics we prefer to live by.

Alison Blunt and Robyn Dowling remind us that home is a place but also an idea and an imaginary (2007, p. 2), imbued with feelings, whether positive or negative. Where we live may not automatically be home but our sense of home can be extended to other places through personal relations and belongings. Home is about place, context and relationship (p. 3). Home is a site and a set of meanings and emotions (p. 22), a relationship between the material and the imaginative realms.We know what home is when we find it. Many of those joining religious groups claim they have finally 'come home'. We have found where we feel we belong.

In turn, I suggest that home is sometimes what we can make of what we are given. We may feel a need to have that sense of belonging wherever we are. Even if we have very few possessions, we may arrange them around us in way that marks territory or offers a pleasing pattern. Cyclist Mike Carter talks of the joy of unpacking his panniers at the end of the day, getting everything into its right place inside his tent. He falls in love with his tent over the course of his journey. It becomes far more than a place to sleep but his 'mobile house', his 'continuity' (2012, pp. 287–8). On very lightweight cycle journeys, even a night in a plastic bivouac bag in a bus shelter or under a hedge became home for me, partly because I needed it to be. However we travel, we want to feel as 'at home' as possible. We want to be within our 'comfort zone'. The challenge is in the degree to which our desire to replicate at least a sense of home excludes anyone else or closes us off to the very people we may have travelled to meet.

The advent of wheeled luggage has allowed us to take more of 'home' with us to reassemble at our journey's end, or at least at the end of that day's journey. The whirr of roller-bags is a routine sound in the airport and is now the new sound on the streets. Why only use wheels when flying? Why carry bags when we can pull them? Why carry less when we can carry more? We take with us from our stable life the 'means to create' to the level we want or need to, and other things to help us feel more comfortable in our new location. We may indeed feel dislocated rather than just differently located. We may prefer our own toothbrush to the one a hotel can provide. We may travel with photos, favourite clothes, our devices. They allow us to minimize the difference between what we have left behind and where we find ourselves.

In David Lodge's novel *Paradise News*, identical hotel rooms are called 'antiseptic' (1991, p. 265), but hotel and motel rooms are, for me, exciting in their semi-spartan nature. Meaghan Morris talks of the motel as pause, a room on a network, like a transit lounge (1988, p. 41). They are staging posts, places to gather oneself and to ready oneself for the next part of the journey. Nice ones speak to me of space and light. Alain de Botton celebrates them as they are: 'uncluttered with our domestic needs and undone jobs. They even provide pads for the midnight thoughts and inspirations' (2002, p. 59). These rooms help us to be 'away' because there is nothing within them that requires work. The laundry has been done and the cleaning done. These rooms represent a blank canvas on which to overlay our version of home. We can move things around, lay out our possessions, optimize our use the space. The longer we are staying, the more effort we may put into this. We may unpack more, or even totally, if we are there more than a night.

Daniel Miller, in his book *Stuff*, talks of how, when we move between places, we realign or 'repair' the representation of our identity, how we want to be seen (2010, p. 98). This is important to our sense of agency even if we never fully resolve how we represent who we are. Unpacking in a hotel room and arranging our possessions is about this repairing of ourselves after the journey. It is about regaining a face after the anonymity of travel.

We create a personalized space from which to wander forth. It becomes a place to come back to, a temporary home, a bit of ourselves or a place we can call our own in a new town or country. We have a key and the right to the space for as long as we have paid for it and its symbolic and real value/capital is huge if we find ourselves in very foreign parts. The room itself will probably have its own systems of distraction, perhaps an internet connection or TV. If there is room service or we can have food delivered, we never even need to leave it. In a way, we are engaged here in our own version of McDonaldization (see Chapter 2), whereby we maximize reliability and repeatability in pursuit of our goal – to feel safe. We create a personal isolation to feel less 'at sea' in the new place in which we find ourselves. We isolate in our own qualified way to ease the sense of isolation or difference we may feel as we walk the streets outside. As we get to know a place better and feel more comfortable in it, make a return visit for example, we may buy a cheaper room, needing less of it.

On holiday in an exotic location, where perhaps we do not share the language or cultural knowledge to blend in or fully enjoy all that is happening around us, we may even opt to have others mediate the foreign for us. We may decide to take the tour bus with commentary in our own language. We let others decide what the tourist highlights are. It may be that a managed safari is 'sanitized wilderness' but given the dangers of wild animals in a foreign location, we are happy to pay to be separated from the challenges of engagement: 'The tourist pays for freedom, the right to disregard native concerns and feelings, the right to spin their own web of meanings' (Bauman 1993, p. 241). What view of the world is given us by those who arrange our travel? How much contact are we allowed to have or do we feel safe to take? What has travel become when it is sold to us in special newspaper supplements for increasingly short snatches of time, guided and guarded by the travel companies?

Whatever the answers, we continue to pay for safety and a sense of well-being. We also pay for comfort. Those without so much money trail around foreign cities, often needing to carry all their belongings with them. These travellers, for example those who lug huge rucksacks, have to engage more with local life as they have no financial choice. They also may see less as being 'moved elsewhere' by train or bus may be more comfortable than walking with the weight upon their back, or spending another night in the town square counting the hours until sunrise. I have had many occasions of being overladen and overdressed for the climate and just wanting to move on. The journey then becomes the security, and the stated goal. Robert Louis Stevenson wrote: 'I travel not to go anywhere, but to go. I travel for travel's sake. The great affair is to move' (1909 [1879], p. 68). It may be the 'great affair' or just weariness and discomfort that drives us on.

With or without a hotel room, the process of travel can become the fixed point, the place we feel least fearful. In the film *Up in the Air* (2009), George Clooney plays Ryan Bingham, someone who prefers movement to stability. He sees the airport as his home environment, inveighs against the baggage of relationship and dependence. He states: 'Last year I spent 322 days on the road, which meant I spent 43 miserable days at home.' When he becomes the seventh person to reach ten million air miles, he is asked on board the plane he is on at the time where he is from, and he simply answers, 'I'm from here.' We make our homes even in aeroplanes and create temporary stability. Twelve hours on a plane may seem a challenging prospect but so is the dislocation of getting off at the end of the flight. Each transition can be emotionally costly: from airport lounge or railway station to plane or train; disembarking; finding somewhere to stay. Even returning home may require 're-entry' time as patterns of life change. As a weekly commuter, I make the numerous transitions from home, to travel, to work and then back again each week. The places of transition for travellers are no longer the great railway stations that Schivelbusch describes but the internal and psychological ones as we go. These transitions are about needing to negotiate identities afresh, even when the process happens every week.

What hope might we have to really meet people who are outwardly very different from ourselves? How might we meet that great curiosity within all of us to learn about 'the new'? Do we think we really want to? One of the ways the systems of travel, described in Chapter 2, have evolved is that they suit us psychologically. We want to be taken elsewhere comfortably and predictably and brought back again too.

Usually, whatever the stated purpose of our time away, to see the Pyramids, swim with dolphins or to eat at a particular restaurant, we want to be 'away'. It is a 'break'. In most travel, it is flight from our everyday lives. Robyn, in *Nice Work* by David Lodge, flies above the everyday early one morning:

> Sunlight flooded the cabin as the plane changed course. It was a bright, clear morning. Robyn looked out of the window as England slid slowly by beneath them: cities and towns, their street plans like printed circuits, scattered over a mosaic of tiny fields, connected by the thin wires of railways and motorways. Hard to imagine at this height all the noise and commotion going on down there. Factories, shops, offices, schools, beginning the working day. People crammed into rush-hour buses and trains, or sitting at the wheels of their cars in traffic jams, or washing up breakfast in the kitchens of pebble-dashed semis. (Lodge 1989, p. 269)

We travel for pleasure, to enter a space where 'some of the rules and restrictions of routine life are relaxed and replaced by different norms of behaviour' (Urry 1995, p. 17). We want different routines, different skies, and different food. We also crave elements of the familiar. The plane may become, in certain overseas settings, the closest we get to what we are used to. In this scenario, it takes on a huge symbolic and emotional value. We don't want the 'different' to be too different.

We want the hotels to be there at the other end of the flight, resembling what we are used to. If there is a Burger King restaurant (or three!) in Beijing, Beijing becomes less 'foreign'

(Urry 1995, p. 150). 'In a world in which self-identity and place-identity are woven through webs of consumption, what we eat (and where and why) signals, as the aphorism says, who we are' (Bell and Valentine 1997, p. 3): we are westerners abroad.

We may want a McDonaldized western style of accommodation so we know what to expect and get our expectations met. We want access to familiar food, at least some of the time. We may want a 'resort complex', fenced in and self-sufficient, so that we are spared engagement with 'the other', the unknown, and all that we may be nervous of. Who of the local people do we really meet and in what capacity? What is the relationship between us as holiday makers and the people who make our stay there possible? What we do we really gain of local culture in such a place? Maybe we did not go to meet local people or learn of their ways. Perhaps we went because it is cheap and sunny. It is 'away' but not too 'away'. It is a time away from all the everyday worries and post and telephone calls, and work, and whatever else we are dealing with at home, somewhere 'removed'. At the same time it is familiar enough for us to enjoy the interlude.

We may need added self-protection, especially in distant climes, because the reality of travel is not always what we anticipate. Primed by the brochure or our own reservoir of imagination, we may instead never find the destination of our daydreams. Empty beaches of white sand next to azure blue sea are never as empty when we get there. Others, like us, have been brought there. Indeed, holiday brochures are conspicuously empty of crowds. Alain de Botton, arriving in Barbados, was unprepared for the airport: 'in anticipation, there had simply been a vacuum between the airport and my hotel' (2002, p. 13).

I had no thought of and now protested inwardly at the appearance of, a luggage carousel with a frayed rubber mat, two flies dancing above an overflowing ashtray, a giant fan turning inside the arrivals hall, a white taxi with a fake leopard-skin-lined dashboard, a stray dog in a stretch of waste land beyond the airport, an advertisement for 'Luxury condos' at a roundabout, a factory called 'Bardak Electronics', a row of buildings with red and green tin roofs, a rubber strap in the central pillar of the car upon which was written in very small print 'Volkswagen, Wolfsburg', a brightly coloured bush whose name I didn't know, a hotel reception which showed the time in six different locations and a card pinned on the wall nearby that read, with two months' delay, 'Merry Christmas'. (Ibid.)

The more 'away' we are, the more different the local culture is from our own, the more we may crave segregation. Our anticipation fed by brochures and idealized images can come to haunt us as the difference between ideal and ordeal is borne out. We are taken in our imaginations only to the end location, not the transitions we need to go through to get there. In this way too, the journey becomes marginalized in our idea of going away. It becomes only the means to the end. In David Lodge's novel on travel, *Paradise News*, academic Rupert Sheldrake suggests:

I don't think people really want to go on holiday, any more than they really want to go to church. They've been brainwashed into thinking it will do them good, or make them happy. In fact surveys show that holidays can cause incredible amounts of stress. (Lodge 1991, p. 242)

Any cheeriness is, he believes, artificial:

Fuelled by double martinis in many cases, I wouldn't be surprised. They know how people going on vacation are supposed to behave. They have learned how to do it. Look deep into their eyes and you will see anxiety and dread. (Ibid.)

This sentiment is borne out by one fellow traveller who later in the novel comments that 'after a week in Hawaii, I can't wait to get back to Croydon' (1991, p. 295).

As an alternative to total seclusion within our resort complex, we may use the guided tour as a way of managing the new and different, as I suggested above. Susan Sontag has argued that photography is another risk-reducing strategy should we venture out. People 'take possession of the space in which they are insecure . . . the very activity of taking pictures is soothing and assuages general feelings of disorientation' (1979, pp. 9–10). The camera gives us a role and a purpose as well as something to hide behind. Photography can give shape to travel. We are highly selective about what we photograph and may simply recreate the brochure photographs with us in them to show we have really been 'there', that our trip was authentic, that we saw what was highlighted as being important to see. Tourist agencies point out good places to take photographs and the schedule and purpose of travel can be centred on getting a good shot. They become explicit resources to help refresh memories, to convey a positive sense of place and of expenditure, to become a vehicle for the display-purchase of the holiday. De Botton argues that '[t]aking photographs can assuage the itch for possession sparked by the beauty of place; an anxiety about losing a precious scene can decline with every click of the shutter' (2002, p. 225). John Ruskin argued that photography may lose its purpose as an additional way of observation and become rather a replacement: if we have a record, we can regard the reality less (ibid.).

We are 'the other' among those we are visiting who in turn are 'other to us'. As tourists and travellers, we have come to see, watch and be watched. Judith Adler discusses the danger of the brief encounter:

Travel landscapes, once left behind and frozen in memory, are more suitable for idylls than are the spaces in which daily business continues to be transacted. Nonrepeatable encounters with strangers more easily serve metonymic functions, delivering unambiguous exemplificatory knowledge of 'the Frenchman,' 'Italy,' 'the Third World,' or even 'humanity,' than the multiplicity of open-ended and complex contacts of life in a home territory. (Adler 1989, p. 1383)

The fleeting encounter gives us a false sense of being able to generalize, of 'knowing' a race or nation. If we stop to think of course, we know that anyone meeting us would not get a complete sense of our nation, but away from home, every experience can be heightened by its rarity and by the focus on 'the new' that the trip can provide.

However, most of us take tours or stay within our resort complexes. We need to feel safe. When we do feel safe, we may indeed feel able to do more to engage, either with other holiday makers or with the locals. If push comes to shove, however, our altruism dwindles. When the 'Ash Cloud' prevented flights over Europe in 2010, holiday makers fended for themselves, often at the expense of each other, securing the last hire car to drive back to 'Blighty' or negotiating alternative flights without any sense of who might need to get home first. Who counted as 'other' for us expanded to include fellow nationals.

The Myth of the Traveller

Self-defined 'travellers' may see themselves as distinct from tourists, and Patrick Holland and Graham Huggan argue that travel writing perpetuates this myth (1998). Judith Adler concurs:

For centuries, there have been debates on authentic travel practices and their supposed degradation. Early tracts debated the merit of long-distance pilgrimage or the advantages and corruptions of the Grand Tour; current ones often attempt to distinguish between 'serious' travel and 'mere' tourism. (Alder 1989, p. 1379)

Travellers, unlike tourists, are: '"nonexploitative" visitors, motivated not by the lazy desire for instant entertainment but by the hard-won battle to satisfy their insatiable curiosity about other countries and peoples' and 'open-minded inquirers rather than pleasure-seeking guests' (Holland and Huggan 1998, pp. 2–3). Travellers may be away for longer than tourists. They may travel through places rather than to them, or 'go' to somewhere rather than 'get somewhere'. It sounds like travellers may be on a spiritual agenda, rather than a self-serving one. However, I think the reality is different for most. They may claim to be open to whatever they find, but I suggest travellers still want to minimize dissimilarity. If too much is too different, it may be too much to bear.

While cycling with my friend Tim in the former Yugoslavia, we met Martin, who was travelling light. He had an expensive racing bike, no luggage and used his American Express card to buy whatever he needed. He marvelled at the fact we camped and lived off so little. 'What do you do for washing, eh?' he asked. 'Well, Ben doesn't wash, and I swim in the sea,' Tim answered. 'But . . . doesn't it f*** up your hair?'

We were all travelling, just in different ways, with different levels of what counted as comfortable. What represented 'home comforts' differed, as did our travelling identities.

The log I wrote religiously every night on my trip to India tells little of all I saw or felt; it simply recorded progress. There was a destination, and while days waiting for a visa did not cause the alarm it would to someone with two weeks leave, travel can be just an elongated holiday.

The fictional Rupert Sheldrake eschews theories of holiday motivation in terms of 'wanderlust' or 'monotony reduction' and divides holidays into 'holiday as pilgrimage' and 'holiday as paradise'. The first type involves visiting cultural sites. It is a mobile holiday; the second seeks a prelapsarian ideal, is static, may involve using as little money as possible (all-inclusive packages or things signed to the room), beaches, wearing less clothing for example (Lodge 1991, p. 242). Later in the book, Sheldrake realizes that even on paradise holidays, pilgrimage intervenes: visiting the waterfalls by minibus for example (p. 251). He suggests in the end that there is simply a conveyor belt of tourists, taken by road, charter plane, cruise liner, one group leaving as another arrives, like a car assembly plant (p. 334).

I agree. Travel is as much about achieving the goal or task as tourism. It is a different kind of tourism, and travellers, as much as tourists, may pay to avoid local engagement and local concerns. By definition, 'travellers' are generally not stopping, not embedding themselves in a new culture. Rather, we are usually 'entextualizing' (the process of taking things out of context). We cannot help but often take what we see out of context given the limitations of time and language as we pass through. In turn, we are entextualized when we travel, made better sense of by our hosts as 'foreigner' or 'traveller'. Only prolonged engagement could get past this inevitable impasse of representation and interpretation.

On my bicycle ride to India, I never stopped anywhere more than a week. I used known networks of westerners living abroad for mail pick-ups and support. I never learnt more than a few sentences in the local dialect, and I never really met anyone native to my surroundings with whom I formed a lasting friendship. That may not seem a reliable criterion of engagement, but it symbolizes for me that the nature of much travel is about 'passing through'. We do so at the levels of comfort we choose and can bear.

I also travelled as westerner and a Briton. My British passport allowed me great privileges over travellers of other nationalities as I travelled through so many former British colonies. Not only was my travel fuelled by the imperialism of my citizenship but it guided how I saw all I passed by.

Anne Coles and Katie Walsh have compared the expatriate community in Dubai that I passed through on my bicycle in the early 1980s with more recent ethnography. They note the attitudes of the expatriates towards the local community, in this case on the subject of dress:

> The majority of British expatriates, both then and now, view Emirati customary dress, particularly the abaya, as a signifier of seclusion and subordination, and, in so doing, reveal a sense of a superior, emancipated progressive British Self in comparison. Such processes of Othering inevitably have implications for the motives and enthusiasm for cross-cultural interaction. (Coles and Walsh 2010, p. 1325)

Everything is judged in relation to British-ness as normative.

> The availability of foods seen as 'normal' is of great concern. During the second invasion of Iraq, there was much anxiety among longer-term British residents who feared imported grocery products might become scarce and some reacted by stockpiling favourite Western brands, thus highlighting that such items were usually readily available. (Coles and Walsh 2010, p. 1326)

Interaction, or the desire to know more about the host culture, is through the managed excursion.

The excursion seems to fulfil a desire to view an authentic Arabian cultural landscape, positioned as timeless and backward. British expatriates perceive even the town of Khasab [with its one shop] as being insufficient to support a modern lifestyle, so it becomes laughable and yet fascinatingly different. These expatriate excursion practices, therefore, resonate with the colonial practices of exploration. (Coles and Walsh 2010, p. 1328)

As Patrick Holland and Graham Huggan (1998) and Mary Louise Pratt (1992) have shown, so much travel writing still engenders the imperialist perspective and agenda. Holland and Huggan write that: 'travel writing frequently provides an effective alibi for the perpetuation or reinstalment of ethnocentrically superior attitudes to "other" cultures, people, and places' (1998, p. vii). It starts domestically with the differentiation between 'travel' and 'holiday', discussed above, and continues as we are guided in thinking of our next destination. Imperialism in these texts dies hard. Britain is still the centre of its old empire and our culture is still presented as the point of comparison.

Julie Codell's work on the visits by Indian authors to Victorian and Edwardian Britain, 'Reversing the Grand Tour', highlights the difference in values and attitude. The Indian authors were not after self-discovery but information to pass to others back home.

Between British and Indian utopias and dystopias, Indian travelers wrote an atopia, a virtual space, in which they had the authority to criticize Britain and to determine India's future. This atopia was the product of their travel, which made comparisons and judgments possible. (Codell 2007, p. 183)

Codell adds that as well as writing out of this hybrid space, these authors did not write in terms of their nationality, rather their writing is de-territorialized. They write as independent witnesses released from nationality by their travel, open to whatever they find, whether positive or negative.

> Indians often described their return home at journey's end, a moment rarely narrated by Western travelers. Indian travel writing evoked the social transgression that was travel itself, so the return must be narrated to create a literary cleansing parallel to the religious ritual cleansing undertaken by Hindu travelers. The return sutured reader and author and defined the trip's 'success'. (Codell 2007, p. 184)

Home, taken for granted by western authors, is foregrounded by the Indian authors, who need to return from the transgression of travel to the purity of home. It is not that India is better but that the value that is given to travel is less. The travel has function and is finite. It is not travel for its own sake. Urry suggests, in contrast, that western travel today is still bound up with the relations of empire (2011, p. 154). I suggest that travel is still part of imperial agency for those of us in the global north. We cannot easily escape such a legacy.

In summary, the highly ordered organization of leisure through processes such as McDonaldization and Disneyization offer a security in their seeming stability and familiarity. Customers know what to expect and they get what they are used to, now globally. We perform our travel (Adler 1989) and tread the important balance between tedium and security.

Anne Friedberg, in a book on cinema and window shopping, talks of 'the mobilization of the virtual gaze' (1993, p. 3), 'a gaze that travels . . . through an imaginary elsewhere and an imaginary elsewhen' (p. 2). The revival of cinema attendance since the 1970s can be seen as a feature of this construction of temporary alternative ordering (ibid.). For three hours, the viewer colludes to be somewhere else, elsewhere and elsewhen, before returning to safe tedium, 'the boredom and meaninglessness of routine, everyday existence' (Bryman 1995, p. 176). Thinking, feeling, and participating can be sidelined. We sometimes aspire to the same distraction when travelling. We want to be somewhere else but our very engagement with that 'elsewhere' may require us to avoid truly engaging with the people we may meet there, whether they are other travellers or locals.

Staying in one place on a holiday may engender closer relationships with locals, especially if we stay away from the usual tourist centres. As someone coming into a new place, we are explicitly the outsider. This can bring opportunities for dialogue. The giving and receiving of hospitality has traditionally been one of the ways travellers have been met. In Jordan, I was often refused permission to camp simply on the grounds that I should rather stay inside with the family. I was shown the kind of openness to 'the other' that I hope we can show as we travel. What is paramount is our attitude as we travel. How open are we to what is unusual, the 'other'? What are our levels of empathy across cultural difference? Do we engage or do we just observe? What are we there for?

Doreen Massey, in her book celebrating space, writes:

When I was a child I used to play a game, spinning a globe or flicking through an atlas and jabbing down my finger without looking where. If it landed on land I'd try to imagine what was going on 'there' 'then'. How people lived, the landscape, what time of day it was, what season. My knowledge was extremely rudimentary but I was completely fascinated by the fact that all these things were *going on now*, while I was here in Manchester in bed. Even now, each morning when the paper comes, I cast my eye down at the world's weather (100°F and cloudy in New Delhi; 46° and

raining in Santiago; 82° and sunny in Algiers). It's partly a
way of imagining how things are for friends in other places;
but it's also a continuing amazement of the contemporan-
eous heterogeneity of the planet. (Massey 2005, p. 14)

Massey is celebrating space and difference but also thinking
about how it is for those living elsewhere. She came later to
see the problematical nature of the globe she spun, how maps
are made by the map-makers and thus denote their interests.
Maps 'map' power. She reflects on the challenge of holding
everyone in mind and how globalization and modernity differentiate and dismiss certain portions of humanity. In this,
she echoes what Kwame Anthony Appiah says about the challenges of cosmopolitanism, discussed in the Preface above.

It seems important to hold on to an appreciation of that
simultaneity of stories. It sometimes seems that in the
gadarene rush to abandon the singularity of the modernist grand narrative (the singular universal story) what has
been adopted in its place is a vision of an instantaneity of
interconnections. But this is to replace a single history with
no history – hence the complaint, in this guise, of depthless-
ness . . . Rather we should, could, replace the single history
with many. And this is where space comes in. In that guise,
it seems to me, it is quite reasonable to take some delight in
the possibilities it opens up. (Massey 2005, p. 14)

Massey wants us not to say that nothing matters but that
everything and all of us matter. It is about the need for the
'conversation', as Appiah puts it, the encounter. For Massey,
the concept of 'space' with its eternal openness heralds hope
for such engagement. In space, anything can happen. It is not
yet mapped, defined and bounded. Rather space is about the
interactions of coexisting lives: it is 'the sphere therefore of

coexisting heterogeneity' (2005, p. 9). Space is never closed or finished, rather it is the 'simultaneity of stories-so-far' (ibid.). It is a place of opportunity for making connections which is ours to take.

Mike Carter reflects how as he spent more time in communal space, cycling and camping wild, home-less, the lines between what was his and what was not blurred. It was as if the whole world was his; not that he owned it but that he had a responsibility towards it (2012, p. 284). The lines of segregation disappeared and the lines of opportunity and possibility opened up.

What if we could travel into such space? It would be scary but so exciting, so inviting, so open and opening. If we really could place our travels and our identities alongside those of others, and engage and learn, surely the way of feeling that connection with the whole of creation would come tumbling into our laps. How are we to travel to maximize this engagement? How do we realize a spiritual cosmopolitanism that nurtures a universal concern for each other and refuses to treat any portion of humanity as lesser? Travel today is essentially 'modern' in its attempts to iron out uncertainties and minimize differences while also continually differentiating between visitor and visited. In the next chapter I suggest we might want to break down the mechanisms of differentiation, and travel with uncertainty, travel in an engaged way.

4

Engagement in the Valley of Love and Delight

We travel, we move, and we 'repair' and re-present ourselves not only as we lay out our belongings in a hotel room, but also as we perform as travellers to those around us 'on the way' and to those we return to. We travel, we cross cultures and we understand our identity to a greater extent in relation to the difference we find, what anthropologist James Clifford terms 'human difference articulated in displacement' (1997, p. 2). For Clifford, travel is 'an increasingly complex range of experiences: practices of crossing and interaction' (p. 3). As we saw in the previous chapter, travel acts as a translation of the traveller's culture into a new context, and thus forms a renewed sense of identity. Identity is created, as Simon Coleman and Peter Collins claim of sectarian religious sects, in vis-à-vis terms (2006, pp. 32–44). In a similar vein, G. K. Chesterton wrote: 'The whole object of travel is not to set foot on foreign land; it is at last to set foot on one's own country as a foreign land' (2007, p. 93). We go abroad, Chesterton says, to learn about our own country. We learn what we are not: 'unknown, distant spaces of adventure are vehicles for reflecting upon and (re)defining domestic, "civilized" places' (Philips 1997, p. 13). As space is open and consists of a series of ongoing inter-relations (Massey 2005, p. 14), Clifford claims that 'location . . . is an itinerary rather than a bounded site – a series of encounters and translations' (1997, p. 11). In this way, we are travellers in our own 'national' cultures too. This may be obvious, say flying between Wichita and New York, or moving among the dialectically distinct areas of Britain.

Our travellers' tales are not only about sharing where we have been but also that we have been there. Ideally we may have encountered and explored some of the kind of space Doreen Massey talks about and we return changed. We may have a greater awareness of the simultaneity of all of our stories-so-far, and a greater appreciation of the unity amid the diversity of humankind. Travel has traditionally filled these roles of education and enlargement. It is said of Benjamin Franklin that his travels allowed him to expand his sense of empathy and help him create his visions of a more egalitarian world.

Many people have had their peak spiritual experiences at moments of despair or crisis. Broken, we find the means to heal. When crisis stops us thinking and throws us onto our emotions, then we can find key spiritual insights and the sense of connection I define as spirituality. When we lose the dualism of self/other so inherent in the way thought objectifies and separates and differentiates, we can find God or Spirit. We find ourselves in what Victor Turner called a 'liminal space' (1974, pp. 13–14), a space of discontinuity and of transition, on an edge full of opportunity. We are liberated from the everyday by finding ourselves in the interstices of worlds. Anything can happen. In traditional spiritual language, we find the mountain top.

I suggest that we may, however, be better off seeking *the valley* rather than the mountain top. This idea comes from Shaker spirituality. The Shakers were a group who broke away from the Quakers in 1747 and were initially called 'shaking Quakers' as they replaced the formula of silent worship with ecstatic dance. In 1774, under the leadership of Mother Ann, the group moved to America. There it quickly grew and has numerous legacies, including stunning architecture and furniture, a number of inventions such as the circular saw and automatic washing machine, a rich theology of gifts, and an emphasis on living 'in the midst'. Shakers, as farmers, have developed a clear sense that the spiritual harvest is to be found in the valley not on barren hillsides (Whitson 1983, p. 258). As a communitarian group, their theology reflects the way God is incarnational in the most collective and abundant sense rather than the occasional and individualized mountain-top vision. It is in the valley where the crops grow. One Shaker hymn emphasizes the valley as the place 'of love and delight' (p. 294). My sense of the spirituality of travel is that we are to find the liminal in the valley place, not the mountain top. The spiritual high of the mountain top is about achievement, rarefied states, the self, isolation, a personal intimacy with the Divine. Down in the valley, the whole of life resides. It is where things grow and die, it is about mixing and mingling, feeling the connection that runs throughout creation, the great Love that laces us all together as we walk through the valley of life. It is not about climbing and reaching a summit, a finishing line, but more about everyday modes of motion. It is about process, not attainment. My 'holy moments', when all feels aligned and in its right place, have been in the midst of cities, of teeming life.

This chapter suggests that given how segregated travel prevents real engagement and connection, we should travel in a more engaged way. We should travel in ways less removed from what we pass across and those we may meet along the way. We should not be conveyed in metal cages, segregated from our neighbours and our potential hosts. We need to travel in ways that nurture the community of strangers. We should seek out the liminal in the everyday. We should seek experience rather than follow a checklist of where to go and what to see. We should seek out engagement. This may mean taking our travel plans into our own amateur hands. It may mean throwing the map or guide book away: 'on the road map you won't drive off the edge of your known world. In space as I want to imagine it, you just might' (Massey 2005, p. 111). It may mean throwing away our gadgets. It may mean taking risks. It also may mean travelling by different means, those generally beyond the reach of the systematization of mass travel considered in Chapter 2. I examine below how motorcycle travel can function as an act of resistance but conclude that it is still a separating and sectarian identity, excluding non-bikers. Instead, I focus particularly in this chapter on cycling and walking. Generally we are moved along by trains, planes and cars and we just sit there immobile. The slow and manual labour of movement and its uncaged proximity to all those we may meet along the way, gives it a particular spiritual potential. There is nothing to hide behind on a bicycle or travelling by foot. There is no 'front' and 'back' area: Erving Goffman's terms (using a hotel as an example) for the difference between the way we present ourselves and what is really going on (1963). We are as we appear. And travelling in these anachronistic ways, we pass through the 'under-routes' or 'low roads' and paths of industrialized Britain, often away from the extreme geography of the auto-centric cityscapes. We become part of the world flashed past by the car. I wrote on the way to India:

> The passer-by's eyes can only stare at the sweating reed for a moment, and the cyclist outstares and watches the expressions as drivers drive on to the next corner that they squeal round to go where they 'must be' going. The cyclist is no receding dot; he is a momentary image; a flash before the eyes on one short straight, soon forgotten. And the expressions, rarely a smile – a raised eyebrow, looks of unbelief – are not at the faceless rider but at the bike, the bags.

From within the car, the cyclist is soon left behind. From the bicycle, the event is a longer and more significant one. We hear the noise of the vehicle coming up behind us, we hope they give us enough space. We then see the car pass and carry on. The car driver has overtaken the cyclist and is then overtaken by their next speedy negotiation. The cyclist is made aware of the difference in speed, of not being hit, of having the kind of perspective given by almost, relatively speaking, standing still.

Being unprotected and unseparated from the landscape, I suggest, gives us a greater sense of engagement and connection with the world we pass through. Doreen Massey talks about 'the chance of space' or meeting with the 'accidental neighbour' (2005, p. 111). These kinds of journeys may be slower and more arduous physically and emotionally but their spiritual rewards are all the greater. Alain de Botton claims: 'Awe can take us out of comfort zones into the wilderness of even greater transcendence', and, 'The sense of awe may even shade into a desire to worship' (2002, pp. 167, 168). I suggest the same is true of meeting those whom we thought of as 'other' and finding them the 'same'. We don't often meet accidental neighbours when reaching our destination is seen as more important than the human dynamics around us.

The middle price range of travel is rarely a good compromise; greater outlay for little additional comfort. Money buys privacy and peace, isolation and the ability to forget what we are really about, but a little money often buys cramped accommodation although perhaps coupled with speed. In 'first class', we can escape the process of journey all the more easily. However, isolation counters our human sociability and induces anxiety. Wolfgang Schivelbusch writes that the introduction of the railway compartment brought isolation but also disquiet (1986, pp. 70–9). Compartments had no connecting corridors at first. Being forced into close proximity with strangers and into 'optical and acoustic isolation from the rest of the train' (p. 77) led to silent journeys of anxiety, heightened after Chief Justice Poinsot was murdered in a railway compartment in 1860. The American system of collective travel was rejected as un-European, but connecting corridors were then introduced (pp. 83–8). As I showed in the previous chapter, we now find ways of managing our space in a railway carriage given we don't have exclusive rights to it.

Our tendency to isolation, maintained and enhanced to extreme degrees in first-class air travel, may also 'pass the time' but in contrast, as Richard Fenn has shown (1995), time may not be something we want to deal away too quickly. Even if we describe a journey as 'purgatory', these times of travel that we are 'unable to forget' may be critical to our spiritual well-being. When we find the ideal place, we of course want time to stop. Damien Galgut comments on a paradise he came across in Africa:

> Only someone cold and hard of heart could fail to succumb to these temptations, the idea of travelling, of going away, is an attempt to escape time, mostly the attempt is futile, but not here, the little waves lap at the shores just as they always have done, the rhythms of daily life are dictated by the larger ones of nature, the sun or moon for example, something has lasted here from the mythical place. (Galgut 2010, p. 74)

Galgut likens this to a place 'out of time' or before time, 'Before history set itself in motion, ticking like a bomb' (2010, p. 75). Travellers who have come here have often stayed.

'It would be easy to just stop and not start again, and indeed lots of people have done that, you can see them if you take a little walk, here and there at various points on the beach are gatherings that haven't moved in months' (ibid.). They have stopped travelling but are still not local. They have found that liminal potential of being between worlds.

I suggest that rather than paying for isolation or speed, difficult or slow journeys may be some of the most illuminating. They also, in my experience, build community. Let us travel more slowly, and take longer to cover less distance. Let us travel among each other rather than trying to avoid conversation and companionship. Life is not easy and seems to come full of challenge and suffering intermingled with joy, but scurrying away from the everyday and from each other hardly gives us the support we need to change what we can of its injustices. Spiritual connection is about process, not goal. As Robert Louis Stevenson wrote: 'To travel hopefully is a better thing than to arrive' (1881, p. 190).

Motorbikes

The counter-cultural nature of much of motorcycling has been well documented. Dick Hebdige's work on sub-cultures (1979) featured bikers, and anthropologists like Daniel Wolf have risked their lives as participant-observers studying outlaw groups (1991). However, motorcycling has also been routinized away from its earlier charisms. Helmet laws have dented the freedom that motorcycling has traditionally symbolized and the use of motorcycles as cheap transport has been eclipsed by the affordability of the car. Motorbikes are now usually a second vehicle for those who normally travel by car. Motorcycling retains a sectarian identity and powerful pull for anyone who has ever experienced its joys but it has become largely sanitized.

Might motorcycling be a 'valley' form of travel that builds engagement and community? Anthropologist Jill Dubisch writes of the annual American 'Run for the Wall' motorcycle pilgrimages of Vietnam Veterans and their allies across the USA to the Vietnam Veterans Memorial in Washington DC, 'the wall' (2004). This is a major undertaking, both for the participants, who need to ride in a group for over 3,000 miles, but also for all the towns that the 'run' passes through and who offer hospitality. Dubisch categorizes the annual event as a pilgrimage, as it 'has a sacred destination ("the Wall")', and that it 'combines the individual search for healing and identity with the creation of a collective narrative' (2004, p. 107).

> Through its journey across the country, the Run for the Wall serves to define a 'home' to which veterans cannot only safely return, but in which they can also realize a new, empowering identity. In this sense, it is through movement that participants both create and experience a sense of place and of 'coming home'. (Ibid.)

The event and its mode create a sense of home or representation and consolidation of identity. Community among the riders and their hosts is nurtured by the common goal. The 'movement itself becomes a form of therapy' (Dubisch 2004, p. 115).

Such organized runs, so explicitly orchestrated in terms of healing and homecoming, are rare. Most motorcycling is not done in this way. Many bikers are loners or travel in smaller groups, perhaps coming together at key places or collective moments in their journeys, such as a cross-channel ferry. Boarding the cross-channel ferries has always felt special to me. There is the performance of being hailed into position on the car deck by the ferry worker, lashing the bike, of sorting out what you need for the crossing, using the few hours for food or rest, and driving off the other side, up the metal ramps, carefully on the bike for they can be slippery, and into a foreign place. These points of public embarkation and arrival are critical to the positive self-image of the traveller for they are 'seen' moments, moments when the world looks on and unambiguously understands what is happening. Our destination is invisible unless some sponsorship deal proclaims it on the side of a support vehicle, but it is clear as we get off the ferry that we have come from where the ferry has come from and that we are heading off somewhere else: slowly on bicycle; in style to the classic car rally; morally with a van full of food for Romanian orphans; we know not where. My motorcycling neighbour simply 'heads off'. I have been there. I can imagine him, perhaps disembarking without his helmet on, perhaps in a group of motorcycles, before heading his own way.

The performance of being a motorcyclist is a heightened activity as few now ride bikes and fewer own such machines. At Matlock Bath in Derbyshire every Sunday, hundreds of motorcycles arrive and later leave. In the meantime, bikers eat and chat and enjoy the sense of tribal gathering, but the moments of arrival and departure are key. We walk up and down looking at the bikes, looking in particular at the unusual. My bikes have never attracted very much attention, but on arrival once, folk pointed and my sense of my being a heroic rider aboard a spectacular bike inflated. When I dismounted, I found that it was all because, horribly, I had a dead bird smeared across my headlight.

High revving engines or the slow parade past the massed ranks show off the bike, its sound, perhaps its rarity (each of us of course is equally proud of whatever machine we have, having constructed its status), then pulling in to park where there is space, front wheel in to the kerb. People watch – we give the interest we want from others – unless there is a mistake. If a bike falls over, we rush to help (there but for the grace of God goes me), then walk away, so as not to compound the embarrassment. We will help with mechanical repairs but there is always the assumption of competence. Going to Matlock Bath is very special for those of us who hardly ever go, but the stakes for getting it right are quite high as it is so public. Helmets of course afford anonymity. The ritual of leaving fascinates me.

It is played out as an affirmation for other bikers but especially as a ritual of differentiation or a signal of aspiration for the non-bikers, caught unawares on their Sunday outing or perhaps there to look and dream of what one day might be for them too. The key to the motorcycle is brought out of its assigned pocket in the multi-pocketed leathers or riding suit and the bike, usually now equipped with electric start, and warmed from its inbound journey, is started with a quick stab of a button. Choke adjusted, the bike idles and warms as the rider gets ready to leave. Ear plugs are put in, then helmet put on and adjusted, then inner and outer gloves. Then the bike is mounted, and a signal given to the pillion passenger if there is one. Hopefully they are deft at mounting quickly and do not topple the bike. The pillion may pat the rider to signal they are comfortable and in position. We back out pushing with our feet, revving continually to signal tribal connection and also farewell, and then often head up the road in the opposite way from our route home, turning around when safe, and coming back slowly or in spurts, but with revs usually beyond what is required. The same can be seen at Devils Bridge at Kirkby Lonsdale or at Box Hill in Surrey, but Matlock Bath offers the longest line of bikes to pass by and the best road to do so. Only TT time at Douglas on the Isle of Man betters this setting in Britain, but Matlock Bath also offers the juxtaposition of biker and non-biker, cars to be held up or overtaken at speed, cars for once in a minority. It is the mystical high, the mountain-top experience brought to the valley amid everyday life, and the blend of the two heightens the attention given it by those on the outside and heightens the desired sense of difference by those within it. Brian Phillips uses the term 'parade society', coined by Laurence Davies, to define a community of optimism regarding European civilization, and in particular the British Empire, that focuses on past and future achievement and glory (2004, p. 59). The motorcycles at Matlock more literally parade but there is also a tribal optimism and certainty about how motorcycling as a way of life has both sacred strength and agency.

It is the sense of difference, both real and constructed, that in the end means that motorcycling, for me, does not really offer engagement beyond its own community. Motorcycles are not accessible vehicles and the culture is differentiated too. In spite of idyllic and slow rides with good company in India, Sri Lanka, and Zanzibar, most motorcycling for me has been quick, helmeted and alone. Helmets, the speed that motorcycles travel at and the concentration needed to ride them in this way, ultimately signals them as another form of privatized, isolated and isolating transport. We need to take off the leathers and helmet to really be alongside everyone else.

Perhaps bus travel offers a solution. Long-distance cyclist Dominic Gill writes the following of his time on a bus in Colombia:

Approximately 24 hours on various buses gave me different and perhaps more normal insight into the world of the traveller. You're constantly entertained by a steady stream of food vendors hopping on and off, or sometimes a smartly dressed sales person presenting a well-rehearsed speech about the product they pass around for inspection, a small box of tablets that is – unbelievable as it sounds – able to cure anything from mild asthma to anal fissures. (Gill 2010, p. 165)

This parade of life sounds hopeful in our search for authentic travel to nurture an authentic spirituality. We travel alongside the local people and meet all that they do in their everyday lives. We can talk as we go, if we have the language, and begin to understand what life somewhere else may be like. I remember travelling by train in India and Pakistan with a similar parade of life. I slept in the luggage rack or under the seat, shared food with neighbours, wrote furiously before it got dark. But Gill goes on to show that his bus journey was dominated by the videos played to these travellers to help them 'pass the time': 'These colourful characters, changing at each stop, operate on a reliable backdrop of Steven Seagal, or perhaps Arnie, fighting highly skilled Chinese gentlemen on the wobbling television at the front of the bus' (ibid.). Moreover, Gill, coming from time on his bicycle, felt isolated from the world he was being taken through. Sights and sounds from outside the bus eluded him:

> Outside, people with no voice look up at you and rivers go tumbling silently under bridges below your feet. In fact, there is a whole hilly landscape of life, people, villages, sounds and sights that the bus traveller only experiences in fast forward, with the monotonous drone of the bus clanking through its gears as the soundtrack. (Ibid.)

My experience of being on the overcrowded bus in Kenya was certainly more 'in the valley' of life than if I had taken a taxi to the airport, but no less segregated. I struggled for physical well-being and exchanged a few words only with the conductor. It was not about connection and community. I found more community in an Egyptian truck driven by someone I likened to Dean Moriarty, where a shared love of music allowed us to transcend the language barrier.

> In a truck, a few minutes of wonderful absurdity: 'gyptian Jazz blares at us, our over-the-hill Dean Moriarty drives with no hands and clicks his fingers, Tim joins in with a roll of the eyes and the shake of the head and the driver's boy sits grinning with an orange duster over his head.

When the tune ended, however, we resorted to staring at the road ahead, silenced by our lack of a common tongue. The lack of language is a problem however we travel but the speed of a motorized vehicle heightens the sense of destination-as-goal and in turn compounds the lack of real connection. In the end, buses, or trucks, like trains, are versions of the iron cage. They allow us to make connections within our vehicles but not to make that connection between traveller and the people and land we travel among. We need to look at forms of transport that are uncaged, quieter and slower.

Cycling

After Dominic Gill's time on the buses, he comments:

> The attractiveness of bicycle travel struck me then more than ever before. No windows blocking out life's real accompaniment. No travel-induced sleep causing you to miss the small stand selling bright, shiny mandarins or mouth-watering fruit juice. From the seat of a bicycle, everybody and everything has a voice, a smell, and influence on your immediate future. (Gill 2010, p. 165)

On a bicycle, we stop when we need to sleep or eat. Our physical needs are paired against our desire to move, not conflated as is the case on trains and planes for example. As cyclists, we do not multi-task.

I love bicycles and cycling. The initial draw was that cycling was the only affordable way I could travel any distance from my Cumbrian village as a 14-year-old. That year I went to see my pen friend in Nantes in the Loire Valley and cycled back alone to St-Malo. Aged 15, I caught the ferry from the top of Scotland to Iceland, caught a bus to Lake Mývatn and then cycled back over the following week to the ferry port. Aged 17, I left Carlisle and arrived in Bombay seven months later. This was a cheap way to travel. The trip to India, some 7,000 miles, cost under £1,000 (albeit at 1981 prices), half of which was on flights and ferries. Such trips were relatively rare then but I followed in a long line of pedalling explorers such as Dervla Murphy, who cycled from Ireland to India in 1965; Louise Sutherland, whose first trip was based on the way the wind was blowing, and who later went on to cross the Amazon by bicycle; and Ian Hibell, who cycled mainly for 40 years and who first crossed the Darrien Gap by bicycle. Nick Sanders, who later also moved to motorcycles, was just completing his round-the-world record attempts at the same time. Okhwan Yoon has been circumnavigating the globe since 2001 for world peace as a cycling equivalent of Peace Pilgrim, and-long distance cycle journeys are fairly common. The wisdom of travelling by bicycle seems to have caught on.

The bicycle is relatively simple technology. Given the spares, everything can be fixed at the side of the road. It is also a form of transport that is almost universally accessible. Lots of people cycle, whether or not they can afford cars. Some bicycles cost a lot more than others but the basic design of the Rover Safety Bicycle and the Dunlop pneumatic tyre still informs the essence of every cycle today. We need no special gear to get on a bike and pedal away, except in those places where it is now law to wear a helmet. On a bicycle, borders can be crossed with a minimum of paperwork – there is no 'carnet' or insurance to check, little to search – and we can cycle to the front of the queue without suffering road rage. There are no national identity plates: cycling is implicitly and explicitly global. Cycling through Indian villages, many young people on bicycles would accompany us for a few miles. Going by bicycle provides a good balance between proximity and connection with what we pass and the ability to cover some distance. Mike Carter, who cycled around the coast of Britain, talks of the 'miraculous nature of bicycle travel': 'just by sitting on a saddle and pedalling, in the space of a day, I had managed to transport myself to another world, foot by foot, mile by mile, a sense of journey and progress that's just impossible in a sealed car' (2012, p. 28).

We feel where we are: we see the countryside, lifted up above many hedges on our saddles, and we see the amazing skies, as was so often the case in India for me. I wrote in 1982:

> Heaven was seen in the cloud formation that night. When it rained, it seemed to me even more magical. To my right, I could look across the vast open space of fields and people in the fields, into the sinking, but still white sun and see the rain patter down on its angled path. To my left, through a thin row of trees, a complete rainbow presented itself, a glowing contrast against the darkened sky.

We are out in the elements. Distance and weather are experienced first-hand, not anaesthetized behind a windscreen. We stop when it gets dark, usually, and we start again when the rhythms of daylight allow us. In the winter, I would sometimes sleep for 14 hours, maybe as we all should. As cyclists, we are aware of every rise and dip of the road. In the Pyrenees and Alps, racing cyclists keen to relive the Tour de France bring their bicycles by car to ride the Col. They race up and down and drive home. On a fully laden touring cycle, we go up the Col at three miles per hour and down at 15. Bicycles also make it very easy to carry camping equipment, clothes and water, thus avoiding the need to stay in expensive towns. Rarely, on those early cycle journeys, did I ever pay to sleep anywhere. I just asked for a place in a field.

Cycling, we can become friends with our machines. Ian Hibell wrote of his bicycle as a companion, crutch and friend. 'The quiet hum of the wheels, the creak of strap against load, the clink of something in the pannier', was 'delicious' (1984). Dervla Murphy named the Armstrong Cadet bicycle she cycled to India 'with' (not 'on') Rozinante or 'Roz' (1965, p. xi). Mike Carter also talks about the companionship of his machine (2012, p. 95).

The disadvantage is that the bicycle and the bag attached to it need to be looked after. Punctures need repairing or more serious breakdowns taken care of. Experiences of theft deter leaving laden machines anywhere very long or even leaving them at all, limiting all kinds of opportunities. Perhaps it is best to travel by local and replaceable machines. Bicycles can be taken by truck or bus but trying to hitch a ride in a car with a bicycle is impossible. Generally, we are tied to roads or bridleways. The world is nearly but not truly our oyster. Maybe in the end, even the bicycle needs to be left behind if we really want to engage with the whole of creation.

Walking

Walking gives us all the advantages of cycling. Rebecca Solnit, whose book *Wanderlust* is a great celebration of travelling by foot, emphasizes the sense of connection we can find simply striding out:

> Most people nowadays live in a series of interiors – home, car, gym, office, shops – disconnected from each other. On foot, everything stays connected, for while walking one occupies the spaces between those interiors in the same way one occupies those interiors. One lives in the whole world rather than in interiors built up against it. (Solnit 2002, p. 9)

Rachel Joyce has written the fictional story of Harold Fry, who one day decided to set out to walk a personal pilgrimage the length of England. In the early part of his walk, he travels through lanes he was used to driving around:

He . . . must have driven this way countless times, and yet he had no memory of the scenery. He must have been so caught up in the day's agenda, and arriving punctually at their destination, that the land beyond the car had been no more than a wash of one green, and a backdrop of one hill. Life was very different when you walked through it. (Joyce 2012, p. 43)

Freed of the mechanics and concerns of driving and destination, everything takes on a different complexion to him. Joyce continues:

Between gaps in the banks, the land rolled up and down, carved into chequered fields, and lined with ridges of hedging and trees. He had to stop to look. There were so many shades of green. Harold was humbled. Some were almost a deep velvety black, others so light they verged on yellow. Far away the sun caught a passing car, maybe a window, and the light trembled across the hills like a fallen star. How was it he had never noticed all this before? (Ibid.)

Walking, we are uniquely open to the awe and wonder of creation. Stopping is easy.

In big cities, like London, only walking allows us to see everything, to stop and watch or look, or chat to the stranger. Walking, there are literally no barriers between people. We become 'accidental neighbours' to each other. Joyce writes of Harold Fry: 'He understood . . . it was also his journey to accept the strangeness of others. As a passer-by, he was in a place where everything, not only the land, was open. People would feel free to talk, and he was free to listen' (2012, p. 87). Once we understand the essential sameness of humanity, we are freed from all the representations of difference that secular culture feeds us. We can better feel that universal concern and respect for difference that Appiah talks about. Harold Fry finds this:

> The world was made up of people putting one foot in front of the other; and a life might appear ordinary simply because the person living it had done so for a long time. Harold could no longer pass a stranger without acknowledging the truth that everyone was the same, and also unique; and that this was the dilemma of being human. (Joyce 2012, p. 150)

Real and imaginary barriers disappear when we are all on foot. We all go at our own pace, self-contained but connected. There is no 'gear' or 'machine', no technology to service or protect. We only need look after ourselves. We can wander where we want. 'Cities have always offered anonymity, variety, and conjunction, qualities best basked in by walking: one does not have to go into the bakery or the fortune-teller's, only to know that one might' (Solnit 2002, p. 171). Walter Benjamin, who Solnit describes as one of the great urban walkers, talked of the 'art of straying' (2002, p. 197). Before him, Charles Baudelaire defined the concept of the *flâneur*, someone who strolls and observes among the city streets. The *flâneur* is at ease in the throng:

> His passage and his profession is to merge with the crowd. For the perfect idler, for the passionate observer it becomes an immense source of enjoyment to establish his dwelling in the throng, in the ebb and flow, the bustle, the fleeting and infinite. To be away from home and yet to feel at home anywhere. (Baudelaire 1995, p. 9)

Cities beckon the walker to enjoy them and Michel De Certeau called walkers the 'practitioners of the city' (1984, p. 93).

Most cities were born in a time when walking was normative and the architecture reflects this. It is walking that continues to generate the city, gives it life and keeps the city from dying (Solnit 2002, p. 213). As walkers, we represent the public face of the humanity that inhabits our environment, not separated by car or house. The streets become where we engage and co-create. As shops move out of town to serve a car-centric society, the downtown can die. Without people on the streets, life disappears.

The only disadvantages of walking is the weight of carrying our home (or all we need to) and the distance we may cover in a day. However, modern rucksack design has made it hugely easier to carry large loads, and the pace of walking has been heralded as particularly beneficial. Solnit says: 'I suspect that the mind, like the feet, works at about three miles an hour. If this is so, then modern life is moving faster than the speed of thought, or thoughtfulness.' This idea of walking helping our thinking is echoed by the poet Sir Andrew Motion, who said in a BBC radio interview that: 'moving your body around . . . can be very productive of ideas' (2012). Wordsworth was deliberately into 'tramping: there is "a step and a beat to writing"'; feeling a certain rhythm established in your body, 'transmits itself into the poems' (2012). In this case, short bursts of travel aid the creativity afforded by stability. Rebecca Solnit says: 'Exploring the world is one of the best ways of exploring the mind, and walking travels both terrains' (2002, p. 13).

We can argue then that walking allows inward and outward engagement. It, like cycling, is counter-cultural. Solnit claims:

If there is a history of walking, then it too has come to a place where the road falls off, a place where there is no public space and the landscape is being paved over, where leisure is shrinking and being crushed under the anxiety to produce, where bodies are not in the world but only indoors in cars and buildings, and an apotheosis of speed makes those bodies seem anachronistic or feeble. In this context, walking is a subversive detour . . . (Solnit 2002, p. 12)

Walking removes one from the daily duality of segregation and places one into the midst of communal space.

Walking focuses not on the boundary lines of ownership that break the land into pieces but on the paths . . . Walking is, in this way, the antithesis of owning. It postulates a mobile, empty-handed, shareable experience of the land. Nomads have often been disturbing to nationalism because their roving blurs and perforates the boundaries that define nations; walking does the same thing on the smaller scale of private property. (Solnit 2002, p. 162)

The Spiritual Rewards of Vulnerability

Walking and cycling place us in the valley. Walking and cycling maintain the pace of human motion, offering the ability to see and stop, to engage more readily. However, in more and more places, the overspill of mechanization has turned paths and quiet roads into less secure and enjoyable places. Fumes and noise and danger from cars and trucks invades the possibility of being wholly present to these means of travel. 'It surprised Harold how fast and angry cars seem when you were not in one' (Joyce 2012, p. 43).

Travelling under our own steam, we are more vulnerable and this makes these forms of travel less popular, even for those with time enough. They lead us back onto ourselves as the final backstop of safety. We may have phones and GPS but we are typically with ourselves and helped by ourselves when crisis occurs. There are no transport police or air stewards or train conductors to call to our aid. Damien Galgut writes of trekking in southern Africa, walking together, sometimes side by side, sometimes apart, 'always alone'.

> It's strange that all this space, unconfined by artificial limits as it spills to the horizon, should throw you back so completely into yourself, but it does, I don't know when I was last so intensely concentrated into a single point . . . walking on that dust road with my face washed clean of all the usual emotions, the strains and strivings to link up with the world. Maybe deep meditation makes you feel that way. (Galgut 2010, p. 31)

At one level, bicycles or our feet are reassuringly reliable. At other times, a blister or a puncture can stall us at some key moment. A broken bone may mean the end of the journey. Cycling alone through France, a touring tandem passed me as I sat outside a small shop eating an ice cream:

> I waved – the woman on the back, with no hands (on the bars) turned and smiled back . . . our eyes met, shook hands almost.
> 'Ho, where are you going?'
> 'Why don't you come and catch up and talk?'
> 'Why I'd love to.'
> 'We'll see you up the road.'

I finished my ice cream, dived into the grocers, settled my account, once outside stuffed groceries into my front bag, unlocked my bicycle and rode off into the 'afternoon sun' past the whistling girls in pursuit of the tandemed pair of eyes and a real talk. But I had a puncture.

We can become very aware of our physical needs and limitations and we need to become familiar with our bodies and look after them in a way not true of motorists. Food is fuel, and early on in his bicycle ride from Alaska to Argentina, Dominic Gill runs out:

> At about 4pm the next day, in an area of highway where the trees on one side had given way to scrubby tundra once again, I sat heavily on the road, starving but with nothing other than a few small bags of rice to eat and no spare water to cook them in. My strength had sweated steadily out of me and leaked away through my pedals. (Gill 2010, p. 36)

Gill was eventually rescued by begging from a tour bus he flagged down. He made a connection with others travelling in a different way and was able to re-fuel. Thus, as walkers and cyclists, we are opened to ourselves and to the world around us, yet still travelling on and passing through. In our physical and emotional openness, we are both embedded within and yet still passing by the world around us. Harold Fry in Rachel Joyce's novel realizes this:

> There was so much out there, so much life, going about its daily business of getting by, of suffering and fighting . . . Again he felt in a profound way that he was both inside and outside what he saw; that he was both connected, and passing through . . . He was both a part of things and not. (Joyce 2012, p. 188)

This sentiment is echoed by Dominic Gill. He would see the news and not recognize within it the world he was travelling through: 'Every day I would pass a TV showing crashes, robbing and abductions. Either, like a parting of the waves, I was riding through it protected, or the nastiness didn't exist in the volumes we are led to believe' (2010, p. 127). On my long bicycle trip, the ride was considered un-newsworthy as nothing terrible befell me.

As cyclist and walkers, we are not fully a part of the world but also not apart from it. We are in a place of great spiritual potential. We move on the threshold of whatever may be: 'between one's past and future identities and thus outside the established order' (Solnit 2002, p. 51). We present ourselves solely as humans as we walk or cycle, in that liminal space where distinctions break down. Galgut uses a border-crossing as a metaphor for transition:

> He always has a dread of crossing borders, he doesn't like to leave what's known and safe for the blank space beyond in which anything can happen. Everything at times of transition takes on a symbolic weight and power. But this too is why he travels. The world you're moving through flows into another one inside, nothing stays divided any more, this stands for that, weather for mood, landscape for feeling, for every object there is a corresponding inner gesture . . .
> (Galgut 2010, p. 85)

In the end, however, the transition is not real, for the 'before' and 'after' states have already merged through the dynamic between outward and inward flow. All is one. Space, and our place within it, is of a piece. We have made the connection. As we travel, space and time are equally fluid, moments of opportunity, of unknowing. I do not ride along the line of the map and the map does not show me the piece of gnarled tree trunk at the side of the road, the accidental neighbour beckoning me to enjoy some dates. We do not travel to somewhere or an event. As Doreen Massey claims, we do not travel through space, we alter it: what we left half an hour ago is not the same space (2005, p. 118). Damien Galgut affirms this insight:

> A journey is a gesture inscribed in space, it vanishes even as it's made. You go from one place to another place, and on to somewhere else again, and already behind you there is no trace that you were ever there. The roads you went down yesterday are full of different people now, none of them knows who you are. (Galgut 2010, p. 132)

Doreen Massey argues that 'here' and 'now' are never fixed, and are almost redundant phrases (2005, p. 118). We might better use 'fleeting here' and 'fleeting now'. I suggest we co-create our settings.

In this movement across the fleeting nature of space, Damien Galgut talks of the weightlessness of the traveller casting away the life left behind – everything is in free-fall as we become aware of the lack of fixed points:

> The thought of casting away his normal life is like free-dom . . . maybe that is the true reason for this journey, by shedding all the ballast of familiar life they are each trying to recapture a sense of weightlessness they remember but perhaps never lived, in memory more than anywhere else travelling is like free-fall, or flight. (Galgut 2010, p. 26)

We are here but not 'here', as, in that very moment of feeling that to be the case, 'here' has changed. It is very similar to the way mystics have tried to understand God. The less coherent our picture, the closer we are. When we think we know God, we have lost touch with the mystery of faith. It is not our place to 'arrive' spiritually but to travel faithfully. Walking, I suggest, gives us the internal space to do this well.

Two hundred and fifty years ago, in the mid-1760s, Quaker John Woolman came to a similar conclusion: that not only was travel important for his processes of discernment (see Chapter 1) but that the mode of travel mattered too:

'Woolman felt God leading him to travel by foot' (Kershner 2012). Woolman felt that the act of walking not only provided solitude for contemplation but also that he might achieve a greater empathic connection with the enslaved he was trying to help, and avoid temptation 'to unprofitable familiarities' (Moulton 1971, p. 145). Woolman claimed that walking as a mode of travel intensified his prophetic experience while travelling and helped him avoid the worldly distractions of his class and race (Kershner 2012).

Crises often force us to adjust our scope and live in the moment. Late one night in the former Yugoslavia, I was cycling along planning the following day and then, as evening wore on, thinking about a place to sleep for the night. Suddenly a thunderstorm broke and the darkening night made finding shelter all the more pressing. Then I got a puncture and with it, the challenge of fixing it in rain in the semi-dark. My focus shifted from thinking about the next day to securing accommodation for the night, to getting the puncture fixed, to struggling with a slippery tyre lever in the rain. My mental horizon went from the panoramic, out of time, to mono-focal very much in the here and now. In these cases, crisis begets a stronger truer vision of our context, rather than always living in another space and time or even in multiple other times, a hetero-temporality. Vague purposes for life become concentrated into dealing with what has to be sorted first.

On another occasion, a mass of shouting football fans wanted to get onto our two-carriage train. The police wouldn't let them on before they moved all the existing passengers up to one carriage, then they put them on the second. My first concern was making my connection, but then as that slipped by, and a fight broke out in my carriage between rival supporters, for my safety, and getting off the train in the shortest possible time. The frustration of waiting 59 minutes for the next connection became gratitude for release! Our horizons and expectations telescope in these crisis situations and we remap our present as well as our future. Planning the future is a luxury. As walkers and cyclists, we are freed of the timetabled and McDonaldized world of mass transit. Miles can fly by as we walk or cycle as our heads are free to rove wherever we wish. But we are also more often thrown onto our own resources. The uncaged nature of these modes of transport gives us a sense of connection but also a constant need to be aware of dangers which caged transport gives us the illusion of being free from.

When these things happen to us as walkers and cyclists, there are no quick exits. It is not easy to escape the uncomfortable. That inescapability, however, is what gives travel by human power its spiritual potential. Would Paul have met the risen Christ driving to Damascus? Would Moses now go 'up the mountain' in a 4 × 4 and drive away from the burning bush preoccupied with his GPS? George Fox so often walked to find the Divine, and John Woolman claimed walking aided spiritual insight. We still walk to Santiago because we know that there is wisdom in that tradition of going on foot.

Travelling is an inward and outward process, not just about consuming a product. As we head elsewhere, we need to absorb the difference of being in 'the other' place, let it become part of ourselves, let it change us, not just go and come back or buy the straw donkey. Travel is at its best the change or movement that takes place inside as we move outwardly. We can go somewhere to become somebody else. It is about coming to feel a new reality, not just think it: we come to *experience* rather than believe. We learn what it is we are. That change in view allows us to recalibrate everything, understand it afresh. As Richard Rohr has said: 'We do not think ourselves into new ways of living, we live ourselves into new ways of thinking' (2003, p. 19).

I suggest if we are to travel that we need to try and avoid segregation and travel in a more engaged way. As Mark Twain said, 'travel is fatal to prejudice, bigotry and narrow-mindedness' (2008, p. 650). It can feel risky to really travel in an engaged manner but the rewards can be enormous. When we are in danger, and thrown onto the kindness of strangers, our very vulnerability can bring out that sense of connection in others. We help each other instinctively and abundantly when we do not feel threatened.

That was how people were: they reached out to one another, no matter what dividing chasms lay between them – chasms of geography, and nation, and language; in spite of all these, people could still look at others and see that we were all the same, at least in those things that mattered, those things of the spirit, of the heart – human things. (McCall-Smith 2010, p. 18).

Mostly we live in the valley, but we are so boxed in and hived off that we do without the sense of connection. We avoid the kindness of strangers through technological proficiency. We try to make the humanity of the human race redundant and we escape the emotional hardship of the disconnect by escaping elsewhere on holiday to similarly isolate ourselves. Walking and cycling are not magic cures. We can find isolated paths and tracks and not talk or stop when we meet others along the way. However, the longer we are away from our cages, free, the more we may find we want to reach out. The more we may see the connection between the whole of creation. Travel could then take on a human element and a spiritual one. The challenge is how we can do that in the everyday and whether we need to go away at all to reach that inward place of insight.

5

Travelling Home

Evelyn Waugh famously wrote of travel: 'I don't believe . . . that people would ever fall in love or want to be married if they hadn't been told about it. It's like abroad: no one would want to go there if they hadn't been told it existed' (1947, p. 115). For all I have argued that travel is now commodified and routinized, I believe Waugh is wrong. Travel can be enchanting and illuminating. Modern travel is not just the consequence of a marketing exercise. We may often travel in segregated and isolated ways, wrongly believing the ends justify the means, but we also have plenty of choices to make our travel enhance and reflect our spirituality. Travel can feed our souls and enlarge our vision. Augustine is said to have claimed: 'The world is a great book, of which they that never stir from home read only a page' (Fielding 1824, p. 216). Indeed, we may need to encourage each other to travel more. As the Sea Rat tells Ratty in *The Wind in the Willows*:

Take the Adventure, heed the call, now ere the irrevocable moment passes! Tis but a banging of the door behind you, a blithesome step forward, and you are out of the old life and into the new! Then some day, some day long hence, jog home here if you will, when the cup has been drained and the play has been played, and sit down by your quiet river with a store of goodly memories for company. (Grahame 1995, p. 195)

Even if we are not bound for long adventures or meandering journeys on foot or bicycle, time away to repair ourselves is crucial. The claim that 'I need a holiday' is not just a response to advertisements telling us so but an insight into how a break with routine allows us time to refocus our perspective and re-gather our energies for what lies ahead. Maya Angelou writes:

> Each of us needs to withdraw from the cares which will not withdraw from us. We need hours of aimless wandering or spates of time sitting on park benches observing the mysterious world of ants and the canopy of tree tops.
>
> If we step away for a time, we are not, as many may think and some will accuse, being irresponsible, but rather we are preparing ourselves to more ably perform our duties and discharge our obligations.
>
> When I return home, I am always surprised to find some questions I sought to evade had been answered and some entanglements I had hoped to flee had become unraveled in my absence.
>
> A day away acts as a spring tonic. It can dispel rancor, transform indecision, and renew the spirit. (Angelou 1993, pp. 138–9)

The fact that so many of us have such difficulty with the process of coming home shows that travel still takes us 'somewhere else' inwardly as well as outwardly. I am always a little disheartened about the return journey. Flying back from the USA, for example, I find myself at the departure gate feeling dislocated as my days of ever moving onward come to an end. I am leaving the safety of the journey for the transition back to the reality of my regular work life, and as assuaged as that is by the joy of going home to my family, it is the end of those travels. I find myself no longer a minority but suddenly immersed in a sea of familiar accents. These are 'my people', and I need to fit in or not, affirm or contradict what I hear. Tired out by an overnight flight, the journey further pales as the plane circles in rain clouds around the diminutive suburbs of Manchester below. De Botton feels the indifference of the city he returns to towards all he has experienced while he was away. It hasn't made a difference to anything. He has been changed, but the city remains unmoved: he writes, 'I felt despair to be home' (2002, p. 252). Mike Carter talks of the end of family holidays being cast in 'the dark shadows of re-entry' (2012, p. 310). Only those who keep travelling avoid the challenge of return.

We are no longer 'elsewhere' but back amid the familiar, the unexotic. It is good to be away. It breaks routines. It may give us luxury we don't have at home, such as a hire car, or sunshine, access to a beach or swimming pool, exotic food, cheap prices, friends or family we rarely see. Vicarious travel or travel by computer does not work in the same way. Meetings by Skype are not the same as face to face encounters. They offer hollow transactions prone to technological breakdown. Seeing the world on a computer doesn't mean we don't want to visit places and see sights first-hand. If anything, the globalization of the local through the internet brings it closer and makes it seem less foreign and more accessible. The place is there on the screen. We know what it looks like. All we need to do is open another tab and we can arrange how to get there. So I am not suggesting that we should not travel or that we are duped if we do. I simply suggest we travel mindfully.

As such, this final chapter looks at motivations for travel, how we might match our travelling and our sense of 'call', how we may find what we seek elsewhere on our very doorstep, and how in the end what matters most, spiritually speaking, is the degree to which we can find and nurture community and the sense of connection that accompanies it. We can travel with parts of 'home' with us or travel towards and out from home wherever we eventually find it.

Compulsive Travel

I wrote at the beginning of this book that I love travel. I sometimes say that I have been called to a vocation of motion. The urge to go away, and the excitement I feel on hearing the journeys of others, or looking at a map, has diminished only slightly over the years. I have been lucky in having so many opportunities to go to so many places. For the landlocked ex-sailor who Mike Carter met on his cycles, the call was a frustrated one: 'Travel's a bugger when it's in your blood' (2012, p. 135). Others have indicated that they hoped to get rid of the desire to explore. Dominic Gill writes in this way:

> I suppose I'd hoped this journey might have purged my system of craving for the new and exciting. One big adventure to sate my appetite and allow me to 'settle down' and enjoy the life of 'grown-up'. Even before the British Airways flight lifted me off Argentinian tarmac to fly home, I realised I had been naïve. (Gill 2010, p. 284)

If some of us are called to travel and others not, then what seems most important is our motivations. Mike Carter talked of travel being a hardwired response when life delivers a blow:

> I was 13 when my parents split up. I took to the railways, sleeping on trains and station platforms, sometimes staying away from home for several days at a time. If it wasn't trains, I'd get on my bicycle and just ride for hours and hours. Where I went wasn't important, as long as I was moving. When my mum died a few years later, I travelled the world, working odd jobs, always looking for the next thing. When my short marriage broke down, I took off on a

motorbike. Movement seemed to be the hardwired response when life delivered a blow. (Carter 2012, pp. 5–6)

Do we simply take flight when faced with plight? Are we searching for something? In Sharon Butala's novel *Upstream*, an experienced traveller, Alex, reflects on her many expeditions:

I was looking for something, I guess. What is it people are looking for when they travel? . . . You think somehow you can master the world, hold it there, in the palm of your hand . . . but the same . . . abyss . . . between you and the . . . meaning of things . . . is always there. (Butala 1991, pp. 39–40)

Does travel take on an internal logic and rhythm of its own, so we travel to keep travelling? In the film *Up in the Air* (2009), Ryan Bingham's job is to fire people for managers who do not wish to do it themselves. Economic downturn is good for business. From his life of movement and his aspiration to freedom from emotional dependency, he destabilizes the dependencies of others as he tells them they are no longer employed. Ryan Bingham's home is barer than a hotel room, and he tells us that he spent only 43 days there the previous year. It is not a place that shows any sign of personality. His identity is in his elite status as a traveller, avoiding check-in queues with privileged status as he collects air miles for every purchase, and negotiating security checks with well-practised ease. His packing is equally practised and he claims he is 'home' when travelling: 'moving is living' he states, 'The slower we move, the faster we die.' While others travel to find themselves, it is as if Ryan Bingham travels to lose himself. His sister claims he lives in a 'cocoon of self-banishment' and charges him in a phone conversation with being 'isolated'. Talking from a busy airport terminal he retorts 'Isolated?

I'm surrounded.' He begins an affair with a woman named Alex, and they meet at different airports in their travelling work lives. He tries to visit her at her home one day to find she is married with family. She chides him later for getting too close to her 'real life' and tells him that he is 'an escape', 'a parenthesis'. Both characters use travel to avoid the challenges of stability.

Damon Galgut talks of becoming a perpetual traveller simply through finding himself in acute anxiety wherever he is:

> The truth is that he is not a traveller by nature, it is a state that has been forced upon him by circumstance. He spends most of his time on the move in acute anxiety, which makes everything heightened and vivid. Life becomes a series of tiny threatening details, he feels no connection with anything around him, he's constantly afraid of dying. As a result, he is hardly ever happy in the place where he is, something in him is already moving forward to the next place, and yet he is also never going towards something, but always away, away, away. This is a defect in his nature that travel has turned into a condition. (Galgut 2010, p. 15)

For Galgut, travel is the way to avoid the present, the 'here and now'. It makes the terrors of the present moment seem to disappear as the mind, and then the body moves on to the next context. It is 'moving away from' rather than a 'heading towards'. No connection is made anywhere: motion is the only aim and salve. The sociologist Pierre Bourdieu coined the term 'habitus' to refer to the way our social actions can become routinized and deeply internalized (1977, p. 32). In other words, the things we do automatically without thinking. For Ryan Bingham and Damon Galgut, travel comprises their habitus. They travel routinely, 'instinctively', without questioning. What I want us to do is travel less automatically and less routinely. I want us to weigh each journey, discern its value, and enjoy its process. We have plenty of tools in our spiritual traditions.

Crossing, Dwelling and Discernment

In his book, *Crossing and Dwelling*, Thomas Tweed understands religious practice in terms of movement or travel across both place and time (2006, p. 6). Religious ritual, such as the Christian Eucharist, moves us into another time – the future – and into another place, an intimacy with God. Catholic convert Scott Hahn highlights this from his own devotional perspective: 'In the earthly liturgy we share in a foretaste of that heavenly liturgy' (2003, p. 11). On a personal level, Hahn writes: 'As I saw the priest raise that white host, I felt a prayer surge from my heart in a whisper: "My Lord and my God, that's really you!"' (p. 8). After the rite, we are moved back into the present and out of that intimacy with God.

Religions then, for Tweed, are about the construction of internal and external landscapes and maps for their adherents (2006, p. 61). Religions help us make homes and cross boundaries (p. 54) and spirituality, for Tweed, is inherently about 'dwelling and crossing': 'religious women and men are continually in the process of mapping a symbolic landscape and constructing a symbolic dwelling in which they might have their own space and find their own place' (pp. 73–4). In other words, religions tell us how to live or dwell in terms of body, home, homeland, cosmos; they offer dietary rules or sexual morality for example. They also tell us how to be nomadic, to negotiate space and spaces. Religions also tell us how to 'cross' (pp. 76–7), whether in terms of terrestrial crossings including pilgrimages, or corporeal and cosmic crossings (p. 92). Tweed writes: 'Religions . . . involve finding one's place and moving through space' (p. 74). Echoing Doreen Massey's view of the here and now within the opportunity of space, Tweed says that religions are partial and are 'continually redrawn sketches of where we are, where we've been, and where we're going' (ibid.). Religions help us understand and know where we are meant to be and where we are headed. They offer us a guidebook for both stability and motion, for the close and the distant. As spiritual people, we move between the distant horizon and the intimacy of the here and now, between now and then, inward and outward, absence and presence, and we understand those journeys in terms of the religious traditions we are part of. We can see that the journal accounts of George Fox and John Woolman mentioned in Chapter 1 display the inherent spiritual connection between dwelling (stability), and crossing (or travel). Religion is about movement and motion, it doesn't just include it from time to time. Therefore, it is all the more important that those of us who want to enhance our spiritual life get that movement right. We want our movement to be authentic, we want our travel to be congruent with what we are called to do and how we are called to live.

In this way, we can see that the very notion of 'call' is part of the guidebook that the Christian tradition, for example, offers us. In Paul's first letter to the Corinthians, chapter twelve, he explains that we all have different gifts, each equal, however mundane, to the other. What is important is that we are faithful to the gifts God has given us to use. In other words, that we are faithful to our calling. In these terms, our vocation, what we are called to do, is to use our gifts. As those wishing to travel, we need in turn to ask, 'How do our gifts relate to mobility?'

In a secular society, spiritual gifts are often confused with skills or talents. They become *our* gifts, *our* talents, divorced from a spiritual provenance. The cult of celebrity reflects a society in which gifts have been secularized and in which some gifts are given greater status than others. We need to distinguish between what might be celebrated and what we are called to do.

Shaker spirituality is very strong on a theology of gifts. The Shaker hymn I mentioned in the previous chapter emphasizes their theology of gifts as well as valley spirituality:

'Tis the gift to be simple,
'tis the gift to be free,
'tis the gift to come down where you ought to be,
And when we find ourselves in the place just right,
It will be in the valley of love and delight.
(Whitson 1983, p. 294)

We can define a 'gift' as any ability or need that nurtures community. It may seem strange to think of a need as a gift but the gift of offering a need allows the gift encompassing an ability to be fulfilled. What often takes time is for us to recognize our gifts.Workshops on spiritual gifts often conclude with people identifying their gifts and taking or being given a 'gift name', a name to describe our spiritual gifts. In this way, we can begin to understand our vocation and what we are called to do. We may be called to travel or we may have the gift of receiving those who do. How are we to tell? In the Christian tradition, we can identify at least four types of call. For Mary, the mother of Jesus, there was the presentation of the fact, as described in Luke 1.26–38.

In the sixth month the angel Gabriel was sent by God to a town in Galilee called Nazareth, to a virgin engaged to a man whose name was Joseph, of the house of David. The virgin's name was Mary. And he came to her and said, 'Greetings, favoured one! The Lord is with you.' But she was much perplexed by his words and pondered what sort of greeting this might be. The angel said to her, 'Do not be afraid, Mary, for you have found favour with God. And now, you will conceive in your womb and bear a son, and you will name him Jesus. He will be great, and will be called the Son of the Most High, and the Lord God will give to him the throne of his ancestor David. He will reign over the house of Jacob for ever, and of his kingdom there will be no end.' Mary said to the angel, 'How can this be, since I am a virgin?' The angel said to her, 'The Holy Spirit will come upon you, and the power of the Most High will over-shadow you; therefore the child to be born will be holy; he will be called Son of God. And now, your relative Elizabeth in her old age has also conceived a son; and this is the sixth month for her who was said to be barren. For nothing will be impossible with God.' Then Mary said, 'Here am I, the servant of the Lord; let it be with me according to your word.' Then the angel departed from her.

In the text, Mary accepts the instruction as a faithful servant of God; 'let it be with me'. She does not attempt to negotiate her call. We may find we are presented with a call to make a particular journey and we simply accept it.

A second type of call can be identified in the story of Moses as told in Exodus 3 and 4. The Lord appears to him as a burn-ing bush, and tells him how he is to return to Egypt and deliver his people out of bondage into the Promised Land. Moses is full of objections. Who do I say I am when they ask? Why will they believe me? First, God has to persuade Moses of his authority by turning his rod into a snake. Then Moses argues that he has no voice to act as a leader. God tells Moses that God will act as Moses' mouth, but still Moses protests: 'O my Lord, please send someone else' (Exod. 4.13). God is angry and then says Aaron, his brother, can speak for him. Moses then accepts his call. It appears like negotiation but God's intent and resolve are clear.

In this kind of situation, we may be called to 'go' or not against our own preferences.

There is the third type of call which we can take or leave, where truly we have the choice. We may have the option whether or not to travel. There is the joke about the man whose house floods. As the water rises, he climbs onto the roof and prays for help. A boat comes but he declines help saying God will save him. A helicopter comes but he declines help saying God will save him. Finally he drowns. When he gets to heaven, he asks God why he was not saved. 'Well,' God replied, 'I sent a boat and a helicopter!' Sometimes God's invitations may come in unexpected ways and we should not be closed to them by pride or inflated piety.

Then there is the kind of call where we find out after the fact that we are already living our vocation. This is how I understand the life of the James Stewart character, George Bailey, in the Frank Capra film *It's a Wonderful Life* (1946). Set in Bedford Falls, George Bailey and his forgetful brother run the family 'buildings and loan' in the shadow of the local bank owned by the unscrupulous Mr Potter. George Bailey has a dream to travel the world but each time he comes close to realizing this sense of vocation, life intervenes. He is called to postpone his plans for one reason or another. As he sets out on his honeymoon travels, a run on the bank at the time of the Great Depression sees him handing out his own money to tide people over. Later he needs to face the challenge of Potter's Field (in Matt. 27.7, the Chief priests buy Potter's Field with Judas' 30 pieces of silver), a new housing development that threatens the business. One Christmas, his brother loses $8,000 on the way to the bank. Potter finds and hides the money. George Bailey realizes the shortfall in his company's accounts will mean jail and the end of his business, and he heads out of town to the river contemplating suicide. An angel, Clarence, comes to his aid and shows him what the town would be like if George Bailey had never lived, how all his acts of kindness over the years had cumulatively prevented many falling into hardship or addiction or serving terms in jail. The town in this vision is ruled by Potter and ruined by the effects of financial greed rather than the humanitarian values George Bailey stands for. Bailey comes to see what is most important and rushes home to his family, to find also that everyone has rallied around and raised the missing money. In this way, George Bailey comes to see that in spite of his dreams of travel, he has indeed been living 'a wonderful life'. His gifts have been well used, and he has been living his vocation.

Our gifts are rarely singular and our vocations usually complex. They may involve a number of different kinds of gifts. In Hinduism, the concept of *varnashramadharma* involves four stages of vocation: living as a student, as a householder, a forest dweller and finally a mendicant or sannyasin. However, even within this staged process of vocation, we are able to offer many gifts within each role. In living out our call, the sharing of our gifts enhances the spirituality of those around us as they too are then better able to use their gifts. As John Woolman wrote in his journal: 'to turn all the treasures we possess into the channel of universal love becomes the business of our lives' (Moulton 1971, p. 241).

If we have had the luxury of choosing our area of work, then, like George Bailey, it may be we are already living our call. We may be able to do what we are good at, what gives us energy, what helps others. We may be able to share our needs and abilities in our local communities. We may find we are already travelling to the degree and in the manner we are called to.

A key question for all religious groups is 'What is of God?' The need to differentiate between the spiritual and the secular is fundamental to our sense of knowing what is authentic and inauthentic. In an experiential faith like Quakerism, what is of 'God' or 'Spirit' and what is our imagination or ego? Spiritual traditions usually have practised ways to 'discern' the difference: they are part of the guidebooks religions give us and such processes help us see what is on the spiritual map and what is not.

Quakers use silent worship as the basis of discernment. In other words, we attempt to use the ability to encounter Spirit in the stillness and silence as a way of finding out what we are meant to do or how we are meant to act. Spiritual guidance is available for every decision even if it is to conclude that there is no one right way. George Fox and John Woolman would have been practising discernment continually as they tried to faithfully follow God's guidance in their lives about where and when to go somewhere. John Woolman wrote in his journal in 1758:

> For Brethren to Visit each other in true Love, I believe makes part of that happiness which our heavenly father intends for us in this life; but where pure Wisdom directs not our Visits, we may not suppose them truly profitable . . . (Woolman, 1922 [1758], p. 399)

In the first part of this extract, Woolman states his belief in the spiritual value of travel. 'Pure Wisdom' stands as a metaphor for God. What is important, Woolman continues, is that we experience Spirit, rather than what we may gain from the journey.

> And for man to so faithfully attend to the pure light, as to be truly acquainted with the state of his own mind, and feel that purifying power which prepares the heart to have fellowship with Christ, and with those who are redeemed from the Spirit of this world, this knowledge is to us of infinitely greater moment than the knowledge of Affairs in distant parts of this great family. (Ibid.)

Heart knowledge of the experience of Spirit breaking into our lives is far more important than what we may find out on the journey we have been called to make. Woolman's letters home illustrate this point: they are frequently short and devoid of news but refer instead to the spiritual canopy which Woolman felt clothed by and which he felt also guarded his family while he was away.

We also develop ways of knowing when we have made the right decision. For Quakers, unity is the first sign of correct discernment, and disunity in a Quaker Meeting means that a final decision needs to be postponed until Friends have been able to 'sit with' the matter further. In our individual lives, we may look for the 'gifts of the Spirit' as listed in Galatians 5.22–3. Are 'love, joy, peace, patience, kindness, generosity, faithfulness, gentleness, and self-control' present in the consequences of our decision? We may look for the release of energy that so regularly seems to accompany a rightly made decision. We may find things fall into place like a line of falling dominos. A few years ago, I sold a camper van I had originally bought as a present for my wife. Both of us wanted the other to have the money. We then thought of visiting Australia where we both have siblings (in Satish Kumar's terms, 'love miles'). Our daughter was due to start school, and we needed to go in a few months' time if we wanted to stay any length of time. My work is normally scheduled up to two years ahead, but only one event needed to be rearranged and within two days everything had fallen into place. It felt like a 'meant' decision. When things don't fall into place so easily, and I need to start making umpteen rearrangements to make something happen, I take that as a sign that I may be pushing against what is really meant to be happening.

The ultimate test of discernment for me is to use the Amish question: 'Does it build community?' Amish experts Charles Hurst and David McConnell report: 'In general, if an innovation encourages pursuit of individual interests over those of the church or community, it is discouraged or outlawed' (2010, p. 108). In this case, the trip to Australia was for all of us as an extended family. It built community. Faced with an amazing bargain classic car which would require an overdraft to buy, and which only I would derive any great pleasure from, the answer to the question 'Does it build community?' is 'No'. It puts us into debt, takes money away from things that would enhance family life. While much less interesting to me, I did buy a new laptop to better communicate home with when I am on my travels, as the function and motivation was to enhance community. Last summer I cancelled a personal day out to the Isle of Man motorcycle races because, while I had been greatly looking forward to it, the consequences of going were unhelpful for my family and all we needed to do around the house that day. Not travelling enhanced community and was the right thing to do. Looking for things to fall into place, a rush of energy, the fruits of the Spirit, or the question as to whether the action builds community, are some of the criteria we can use when planning whether or not, and where, to travel. I use the next section to think about finding what we seek through travelling close to home.

Travelling in One Place

Bruce Chatwin noted that the seventeenth-century French philosopher Blaise Pascal felt 'all our miseries stemmed from a single cause: our inability to remain quietly in a room' (1987, p. 161). Faced with 'the natural unhappiness of our weak mortal condition', Pascal argued that 'one thing alone could alleviate our despair, and that was "distraction" (*divertissement*)' (ibid.). Chatwin suggested this need for distraction may be 'an instinctive migratory urge akin to that of birds in

the autumn'. Chatwin claimed that to rediscover our humanity, we have to 'slough off attachments and take to the road'
(1987, p. 162).

> Natural selection has designed us – from the structure of
> our brain cells to the structure of our big toe – for a career
> of seasonal journeys on foot through a blistering land of
> thorn scrub or desert . . . If this were so; if the desert were
> 'home'; if our instincts were forged in the desert; to survive
> the rigours of the desert – then it is easier to understand
> why greener pastures pall on us; why possessions exhaust
> us, and why Pascal's imaginary man found his comfortable
> lodgings a prison. (Ibid.)

For Chatwin, the problems facing humanity start when we
prioritize stability over motion. We are all born to move, to be
nomadic. Anthropologist James Clifford similarly sees travel
as inherent to the human condition. For him, the question
is not 'Why do we travel?' but rather 'Why would we not?':
'when travel . . . becomes a kind of norm, dwelling demands
explication. Why, with what degrees of freedom, do people
stay home?' (1997, p. 5).

But we could, and many of us do, choose not to travel.
We may have reduced economic circumstances but for many
of us stability is preferable to motion. We do not all need to
go away. We may not travel in order to reduce our carbon
footprint. In a context of restlessness driven by western insti-
tutions and seductive symbols of power, not travelling can be
seen in terms of resistance, not limitation. To not travel at all
may allow us to find enchantment on our doorstep. The Zen
saying goes: 'Sitting quietly doing nothing, spring will come
and the grass will grow by itself.' Living locally, we can find
the exotic more locally, and find that the new 'away' is 'here' –
staying put has become rare and exotic. Not going may allow

us to see the world immediately round us with greater clarity and greater vitality and allow us to reclaim our local heritage away from all the standardized spaces and routinized processes that facilitate the mobility of the masses. Do we need to work out what to take away with us and whether we can get there on time? Do we need to engage with airports or motorway service stations? Enchantment is on our doorsteps if only we reclaim what it was we were originally seeking to find by leaving home: 'elsewhere' can be literally around the corner, the Divine in the everyday if only we stop to listen. Alternatively, we may just want to travel less or to places less far away. Mike Carter, destined for Argentina, found instead that he could have an 'exotic adventure' (2012, p. 43) in his own geographical backyard.

Alain de Botton writes that: 'What we find exotic may be what we hunger for in vain at home' (2002, p. 78). It is almost the opposite of home sickness. We are sick *for* something lacking at home: we just need to try to find it there, whether it be peace, quiet, or a break from the everyday. For Damon Galgut's anxiety-ridden traveller, the unknown goal was a 'home' where the anxiety would dissipate, where the unknown that induced such fear could become 'known' and tamed. Eventually he finds 'home':

> By then the little town and even the landscape around it are also connected to him, there is no interruption between him and the world, he isn't separate any more from what he sees. When he goes out the front door now it isn't to catch a bus, or to find another hotel, he walks into the mountains and then he comes back home again. Home. (Galgut 2010, p. 22)

He doesn't feel like a traveller any more. His is a motion which centres on home, not on being always elsewhere. Maybe in an ideal world, our travel may be limited to our commute, and our commute may be limited to walking around the corner or down the road. Matthew Crawford, in his wonderful book *The Case for Working with Your Hands*, talks of how so much of 'modern' office work is isolating and lacks connection with the final product (2009, p. 44). The same can be said of our daily commutes. They become means to a sometimes obscure end, rather than a journey resplendent in its own dignity and process. We just need to get to work and get back again, to survive the ordeal of the crowded train or clogged motorway. These journeys need to be weighed and discerned as well as our overseas holidays.

I suggested in the Introduction that our ability to create is directly connected to our ability to find a stable base from which to create. Creation 'on the road' is not easy and mobile devices for any kind of work usually bear the mark of compromise. Our laptop screens are smaller, our hard drives smaller. Travel hairdryers or kettles are small or less powerful or both. Mobile forges are limited in what they can be used for. We are constantly offered innovation in terms of mobile telephones because their inadequacies demand it. Travelling, that is prioritizing motion over stability, can, as we have seen above, take on a life of its own, but it can also be wearing in its limitations. Even for those of us practised at living out of a suitcase, the chance to stay in one place for a while usually brings relief and pleasure. On my long cycle trips, I adopted a 'Sabbath' once a week to wash clothes and dry them or to fix the bicycle or just to relax as essential to the well-being and sanity of the long-time traveller.

Dominic Gill writes of continually cycling away from stability:

I thought about the two years and two days I'd spent on the road. During quiet moments like this I thought about the people I had met and then cycled away from. While my brain was full of beautiful experiences, I still felt somehow strangely unfulfilled. I was getting close to the end, but my permanent pedalling away from stability detracted from my enjoyment of the present. I experienced a regularly recurring state of regret, and it was completely exhausting. (Gill 2010, p. 253)

As he ended his journey, he reflected on all he had missed 'back home' and what he would be returning to:

I'd left the UK before Gabhran, my first nephew, had developed any memories of me. To him, I wasn't Uncle Dominic at all; I was 'the man on the bicycle'. Weeks back, I'd thought that name had a heroic sound to it. Now it sounded hollow, a little sad, lacking family connection. I walked through the silently falling snow, reflecting on the alternating peaks and troughs of over two years of intoxicating friendships and heartbreaking loneliness that had created an indifference I found unnerving, and I thought it was perhaps time to go home. But 'stability' had a terrifying ring to it. It was going to take some getting used to. (Gill 2010, p. 283)

Gill is facing the transition back into 'stability' that I talked of in Chapter 3. Coming back or leaving is not easy. Points of transition, potentially liminal spaces, are not emotionally empty spaces. Last year, I needed to leave home the day after my birthday. The day before had been so lovely, with a grand meal all together at the end of it that felt so loving it had brought tears to my eyes. Early the next morning I was up at 5.20am, to leave the house at 6am before anyone else was awake, to check-in at the airport by 7am. The thought of leaving home was almost unbearable. Only the necessity of work and the meeting of friends overseas offset the homesickness I felt.

When we have choices, do we really need to go? Do we need to put ourselves through what can be the ordeal of travel? Lucien Freud famously claimed that his

> idea of travel is downward travel, really. Getting to know where you are, better, and exploring feelings that you know more deeply. I always think that knowing something by heart gives you a depth of possibility which has more potential than seeing new sites, however marvellous and exciting they are. (Waters 2010, p. 16)

Nancy Waters, reflecting on Freud's idea, says she thought that after five years in central London, she would be ready to move on, but suggests that becoming 'local' can be as rewarding as being somewhere new. While the unknown-elsewhere promises everything (I think of school trips to rare places and the deep-fried mars bar available only over the border on trips to the Edinburgh Show!), we may find the unknown and unexpected on our very doorstep.

It is not movement that leads inherently to transformation. I know that from my mother's migration from London to the north of England and back again. A new town did not give her a new start, simply an eight-year interlude of cultural and linguistic misunderstanding and much loneliness. As we saw in Chapter 3, our travels need to lie within our comfort zones. We need to be able to translate at least a portion of 'home' into the new settings. Instead of moving away, we could find new settings close to home. Waters suggests: 'Perhaps no matter where you are it's worth asking how much more might be revealed and what rewards may be in store if you stopped looking around for the next adventure and dedicated yourself wholeheartedly to getting to know your chosen city' (ibid.).

Waters suggests that we need to see our environments in new and deeper ways. It is about travelling downward.

Maybe we can think about our relationship with our chosen home like any relationship, where the more time you put in, the greater your reward. There could even be something strangely comforting about the ubiquitous multi-coloured bag shops that line Hackney Road, or navigating heaps of last night's beer bottles outside the George and Dragon on the way to work each morning. Perhaps it's not just about new things to see but new ways of looking. (Ibid.)

Alain De Botton tried to explore his own house as a traveller and then his neighbourhood, seeing it with fresh eyes and without making the usual rush for the means to elsewhere. He took time to listen to the conversations around him, engage with what was going on, as we do when abroad. He gave himself permission to 'act a little weirdly': 'I sketched the window of a hardware shop and word-painted the flyover' (2002, p. 252). He explored locally. The painter Stanley Spencer brought the religious landscape of Christian history to his neighbourhood in his art, rather than travelling the globe to paint it. The last supper was set in Cookham, as was the resurrection, and the ministry of Saint Francis. All these religious settings became incarnated in Berkshire. Mike Carter, instead of struggling with inadequate Spanish in Argentina, set out around Britain on his bicycle and almost immediately traded greetings with women waiting for the bus and talked about his cycle trip with a fruit seller, who ended up giving him a map. He had what sociologists call cultural capital: he knew the culture and spoke the language – as he relaxed into his journey and started greeting complete strangers, he discovered the home he was already a part of. He discovered his own island.

Finding Community

That may make it all sound rather easy. It may not be. Home may not be where we are or where we think it is. In 1990, Edmunds Bunkse returned to Latvia after 44 years of exile:

> I found that it is impossible for me to go home. That is not an uncommon experience in the postmodern world, but it took a journey to my homeland to learn that my ideas about that land and its people were only illusions . . . I have found that a home is more than a national anthem, a beautiful city center, patches of beautiful rural and 'natural' landscapes, a stormy, sometimes utterly calm sea and white, amber-bearing beaches, some festivals, a few friends and relatives. Nostalgia for homeland cannot overcome the passage of time. The journey home was wrenching. (Bunkse 2004, p. 56)

For some of us, we may need to migrate to find home. Anne-Marie Fortier writes of many lesbians and gay men who have had to escape 'home' in order to find their real homes, their more authentic places of identity and relationship (2003). Fortier writes that it can be a multi-motioned journey of arriving, searching and leaving until home is finally located (ibid.). Forces children suffer similar processes of multiple dislocation, moving camps and schools every few years. This can give the sense that no one place can ever be home and lead to the kind of compulsive travelling described above. For Nina Sichel, born of an American mother and German father who was raised in Venezuela and who spent summers in New York, home is not a 'real place' but a 'shifting definition'

(2004, p. 185). Personally, I only ever imagined home was about movement. It was not a place but a way of life. I didn't imagine I could find a community or a stable existence. In the meantime, the very processes of always moving meant that I did not even see what I was looking for. I was like Galgut's anxious traveller, always moving ahead of myself, blind to the awe and wonder around me. I was closed to connection.

I know of many people who have travelled the world in order to find that they are meant to live just a few hours from where they set out. Travel writer Tobias Jones spent over a year visiting communities across the world in search of the ideal place to live. He came back and didn't know what to do next: he felt he was a stranger in his own land. He drew a line under travelling and stayed quietly in his own room. He mused on whether Pascal was right and that we cannot find happiness as we cannot sit quietly in our own room, 'But for the first time in years I was sitting quietly not doing anything and happiness had taken me by surprise' (Jones 2007, p. 190). He came to see the truth of the Zen saying that sitting quietly doing nothing spring comes, and with his family decided to find community in his own neighbourhood.

> It was only once we were static, determined to be still, that I realised how much our manic, modern mobility is a mask for irresponsibility. I decided – rather a daft decision for a travel writer – to give up travelling. We drew a circle with a mile radius from our house and decided that was our community. We were, in some way, responsible for everything inside that tiny circumference . . . We wanted to renounce selectivity and discover that arbitrary community which surrounded us. (Jones 2007, pp. 190–1)

We are called to love our neighbours, whoever they are. Knowing them, however, must surely be a start. As Jones did, we can find the remarkable and the unexpected. Jones found all kinds of allies and companions within a mile from his home, even the kinds of utopian communities he had been travelling so far to find. He worked for the charity Emmaus and found his whole lifestyle and his need to earn, changing. His travelling, in some ways, had not been necessary.

Community is, I suggest, able to transform personal identity into a sense of spiritual connection. In community, we find that spiritual sense of deep connectedness. We find a shared purpose beyond maintaining the community itself and we come to share in the joys and challenges of fulfilling that purpose. We come to know each other in the things that are eternal. We come to feel love between us and the love that threads all of humanity together. We come to lose the sense of what is mine and what is yours. It all becomes ours. Dominic Gill wrote of his cycling odyssey: '. . . slowly, ever so slowly . . . I learnt the real worth of the journey. Company. Sharing. Faith in those around you wherever you are' (2010, p. 85). We learn to love the accidental neighbour. We realize there is no such thing as a stranger. We begin to live with universal concern.

Robin Dunbar's research is pertinent here. He suggested in an article in 1992 that there was an optimum number of meaningful relationships any one of us can maintain (1992). Contrary to the hundreds of Facebook 'friends' we may claim, we are unlikely to ever have more than 150 true friends – those we have stable and ongoing relationships with. 'Dunbar's number' correlates with the Amish guideline that a community should divide when it exceeds 35 families, a rule also applied within Quaker Meetings in the past. If we draw a one-mile radius from our house, is that a first step to finding our community of up to 150 people without the need to reinstall parts of 'home' all over the nation or the world?

Henry Thoreau is someone else who travelled less to find a sense of authenticity. He lived in a cabin in the woods for two years near Concord in Massachusetts. His was a social experiment in simplicity, self-reliance and spiritual discovery. He says: 'I went to the woods because I wished to live deliberately, to front only the essential facts of life, and see if I could not learn what it had to teach, and not, when I came to die, discover that I had not lived' (1995, p. 58). He clears some of the woods in exchange for materials and food and receives visitors but is often alone. He visits Concord almost daily but is also critical of how others are forced to earn their living and how they spend their wages. He claims that they are so entrenched in the demands of the marketplace and commerce, it is as if they are doing penance. The end of his book reflecting on his experiment is critical of conformity and affirms the idea that we need to follow our heart:

> I learned this, at least, by my experiment; that if one advances confidently in the direction of his dreams, and endeavors to live the life which he has imagined, he will meet with a success unexpected in common hours . . . Why should we be in such a desperate haste to succeed, and in such desperate enterprises? (Thoreau 1995, pp. 209–10)

Thoreau is critical of the railways: 'If we stay at home and mind our business, who will want railroads? We do not ride on the railroad, it rides upon us' (1995, p. 60). He sees travel in general as inauthentic and claims 'our voyaging is only great-circle sailing' (p. 207). Thoreau is into downward travel but achieves it through separation. Tobias Jones' idea of community is more embedded in local life and gives us a better model of what we can all achieve.

We see in Waters, Carter, Jones and Thoreau a way in which their perspectives are changed. It may have taken not moving, or moving locally, or moving away, but all of them find the enlargement that we so often seek through travel on their doorsteps. In the novel *The Alchemist* by Paulo Coelho, the treasure that the hero seeks is actually in the place where he began (2006). The Jesuit Gerard Hughes walked to Rome and later to Jerusalem to highlight his concerns and to fulfil his call (1986, 1991). He did not make those journeys to find God:

> The real obstacle on our journey to God is not heat, thirst, blisters, road blocks, or other people, but the inner workings of our own minds, our inherited and unquestioned ways of perceiving ourselves and the reality around us. (Hughes 1986, p. viii)

We need to know what we are travelling for and see how far we can meet those needs through downward or inward travel. I look back at the log I wrote nearly every day of my seven-month cycle journey, and all the journeys I have made since. Have I really had a vocation of motion? At one level, yes, travel is part of my call. But I also know that my call is not about travelling or not travelling. It has been about getting to a place where I can share my gifts. What has changed through all of that travelling is how I am in myself. The trip to India registered so little emotionally. It was not a straightforward jaunt but I just kept persevering until all the physical and bureaucratic barriers had been overcome. I eked out the money, managed time and motion, and succeeded. I travelled thousands of miles but really moved, inside, hardly any distance at all. I returned as insecure and closeted and as fearful of my mother as when I had left. I did not find 'myself' or 'God' or love or enlightenment. My vocation of motion has surely not been to simply pass through places as if they were postcards. My spiritual experience tells me that life, and travel within it, is about far more than window shopping from a bicycle. When my daughter asks me what happened or for tales of the trip, there is little to tell her. Being chased by Humphrey the camel in a Qatari car park; eating too much two days in row at large hotel buffets after weeks of subsistence; being arrested in Egypt and escorted by a police tractor; a dangerous moment on the Khyber Pass; eating *thali* after *thali* in India at a Government Rest House with a fixed-price deal; riding a motorcycle for the first time. The log mentions few of these and then not in any detail. I do not remember huge amounts of pleasure (although a succession of cakes in the Plaka district of Athens with a waiter who could roll his r's to spin out *efferisto* ['thank you'] for ever is a delightful memory), just the need to get to where we said we would get to. As Robert Louis Stevenson wrote: 'Some people swallow the universe as a pill: they travel on through the world, like smiling images pushed on from behind' (1881, p. 110).

I have seen amazing places, I have swallowed the universe, but equally important have been the changes I have made when not travelling. I have found ways to create and be creative. I have discovered the joy of stability and a love of my home country. I have discovered the joys of home. I have come to know what 'home' means and what heart-connection feels like. The inward journey has been more significant for me than any amount of outward travelling, even though the outward travels have allowed me to meet and learn from some remarkable people. Only at standstill have I really embraced transformation.

One day recently I went to London for the day. As always, I found it exciting, full of visual delight, vibrant and intense. It was a place I lived in for ten years and said I never wanted to leave. In the evening, I caught the trains home to Clitheroe. Pendle Hill shone in the setting sun. While I will always be an outsider, from another place, in that town, it has become home. It is the place I want to return to, where I can most be myself, where I can share my gifts and where the most important people in my life are. Maybe home can be anywhere we choose it to be, but it is not an individual choice. Home is where we find and share community, not just identity.

Thus, in the end, we should travel and not travel. We travel to find 'fit' between ourselves and the community we can place around us. We travel to find awe and wonder, connection, and love. We could travel less far to find them and less far when we have found those things. What is important is awareness of motive and process and the degree of engagement and connectedness our travelling allows. It is not about destination but the journey, and it is about inward as well as outward movement.

A recent experience of a journey home after six days at work in Birmingham brought this home to me. I had a train ticket from a station 20 minutes' walk away but as the trains are often cancelled on the local line, I paid an extra £2 to catch a bus to get me to the main railway station more quickly. The bus ride was crowded, frustratingly slow, but it got me to New Street just in time for the 4.20pm train north, and I rushed onto the train triumphant with my success. I even found two seats to myself in the Quiet Coach and looked forward to a relaxing journey. Fifteen minutes later, we had not moved. An announcement told us that the driver had been 'displaced' after 'a significant incident' somewhere else in the network. Finally, we left ten minutes late. I still had six minutes for my change at Wigan, but as happens so often, the delay grew: 15 minutes at Crewe, 20 at Warrington. I missed my Wigan connection and decided to head on to Preston. There I could get to Blackburn, but on this one hour of the day, the Blackburn train leaves Preston two minutes later than

normal and arrives just after the Clitheroe train departs. I arrived
in Blackburn one minute after the Clitheroe train left and had 59
minutes to wait.

I estimated it would take two and a half hours to do the
15 miles from Preston to Clitheroe, five hours in total for the
120 miles from work to home (it took two and a half hours
by car). I was an hour late after six days away and the possibility of seeing my daughter before bedtime was threatened.
I knew I had missed dinner. I suddenly felt tired, sad, angry.
Alcohol was tempting as it had been for those already fuelled
who hung around the station entrance. I thought of catching
a cab but the eight miles cost £20. I thought of catching a bus
but the evening schedules wouldn't have got me home any
quicker than the next train. I decided to walk into the cathe-
dral town. It was 7pm. The chip shop was shut. The Mall was
shut. However, the supermarket, encased in its own arcade,
still showed lights, and I joined the tail end of evening shop-
pers, seeking bargains or spinning out the early evening.

I was full of what I might have done. I shouldn't have
wasted money on the bus ticket. I should have gone via
Manchester where I could have had chips and met a friend. I
could have had chips in Preston, but then again the Clitheroe
train could have been late and I might have missed my change
at Blackburn. I have learnt to always keep going; get as far
as you can on rail journeys so beset by uncertainty. I bought
some food and sat eating my pie and my banana under the
neon lights and in that instant realized again that all was
good. To be there, with other folk, in a place I knew, where
I could claim legitimacy, even if from another place and with
a wholly other accent. Better the bench you know. I could fit
in. When I came out of the arcade, the rain had started; even
on a summer day of unbridled sunshine in London, following
the hottest day of the year so far, it was raining in Blackburn.
I laughed. I was indeed 'home'. I had eaten, that most

important of privileges. As the next train to Clitheroe came in, I knew I would be going home and that I would still get to read the bedtime story. All was well.

What I needed was perspective. I needed to be les focused on the goal and more on the process. In the end, my miniature crisis allowed me to *feel* the situation more clearly. My only enemy was expectation.

Mike Carter reports a conversation with Stevie Smith who set out to go around the world using only human power: cycling and a pedal boat. When Mike met him, Stevie was back in Britain working as the ferryman between Salcombe and East Portlemouth in Devon. Stevie claimed he had found the perfect job. 'There is no promotion, no professional goals or advancement' (Carter 2012, p. 315). That wasn't easy having returned from a journey based on achieving a particular goal and in affluent Salcombe where comparisons are always being made about who does or has what. However, Stevie told Mike, he came to see that having nowhere to go is a 'wonderful release' (ibid.). 'When you discover that every step of the journey is the same. You can enjoy the first step and the last step and every step in between. They're all just as important' (ibid.). Achieving goals may give someone a wonderful feeling but once the goal has been achieved, it is in the past. Either we then have to find another goal or we can learn to take single steps: 'finishing lines are good, but their most important role is to get you over the start line in the first place' (p. 316). As Ursula le Guin wrote in *The Left Hand of Darkness*, 'It is good to have an end to journey toward, but it is the journey that matters in the end' (1969, p. 220).

Echoing Stevie Smith's emphasis on the freedom of ordinariness, Richard Rohr writes:

It's a gift to joyfully recognize and accept our own smallness and ordinariness. Then you are free with nothing to live up to, nothing to prove, and nothing to protect . . . once you know that your 'I' is great and one with God, you can ironically be quite content with a small and ordinary 'I'. No grandstanding is necessary. Any question of your own importance or dignity has already been resolved once and for all and forever. (Rohr 2005)

Free of the need to present self in any inflated way, to 'display' or 'parade' our travels, we can give more attention to the journey rather than its destination. As a Quaker, I worship in silence and stillness, expecting an inward sense of presence to come out of the outward absence of noise and movement. If we give way to just living in the present without thought for any destination or finishing line, presence will appear out of absence. We may not understand what we experience. Spirituality is mysterious and faith, not thought, is its natural companion. When we think we understand the spiritual realm, we are probably a long way from it.

Equally, we cannot know where our expectant waiting will lead us. Martin Buber wrote: 'all journeys have secret destinations of which the traveller is unaware' (2002, p. 36). There is the outward and the inward. What is important is our embeddedness in the present moment, of feeling where we are, and not losing ourselves in books or films or schedules or destinations, or fear of the other, or trying to beat our neighbours to the best seats or by protecting our space. Let us try to be open to everyone and to the moment. The Buddhist monk Thich Nhat Hanh writes of arriving and being home 'in the here' and 'in the now' (1997, p. 27) and commends walking meditation to us:

When we practice walking meditation, we arrive in each moment. Our true home is in the present moment. When we enter the present moment deeply, our regrets and

sorrows disappear, and we discover life with all its wonders. Breathing in, we say to ourselves, 'I have arrived.'
Breathing out, we say, 'I am home.' When we do this,
we overcome dispersion and dwell peacefully in the present moment, which is the only moment for us to be alive.
(Thich Nhat Hanh 1997, p. 29)

Home then is not a place but a state of being, a relationship.
Hanh claims that when we are present in this way, we become
open to the wonders of the universe (1997, p. 52). What is the
equivalent of walking meditation for car drivers? Surely we
can invent it, and one for rail and air passengers also. We can
all practise living in the present moment and travel, or not,
mindfully. We will find ourselves where we are meant to be or
find we are already there. Hafiz, the Sufi poet, wrote:

Making our Connections

This place where you are right now
God circled on a map for you.

Wherever your eyes and arms and heart can move
Against the earth and the sky,
The Beloved has bowed there –

Our Beloved has bowed there knowing
You were coming.

(Hafiz 2003, p. 12)

Thus, I suggest, we may be called to move less outwardly and
more inwardly. Moreover, I suggest an inverse relationship
between the two, as I have suggested there is an inverse relationship between travel and stability and the ability to create. When we stop our outward processes of crossing, we can

dwell. In turn, sitting quietly doing nothing, or creating within a home life of stability, can then lead to inward crossing or transformation. Only when we stop in our outward travels, even for an instant, to give full attention to where we are, do we really connect. In Bourdieu's terms, we can live within a new 'habitus' of travel, a culture of process and engagement rather than destination. We can travel when 'led' or prompted, and when we do travel, attempt to do so mindfully.

The holy is everywhere and we need not go far to find it, but equally we should go nowhere without it.

References

Adler, Judith, 1989, 'Travel as performed art', *American Journal of Sociology* 94, pp. 1366–91.

Angelou, Maya, 1993, *Wouldn't Take Nothing for My Journey Now*, New York: Random House.

Appiah, Kwame Anthony, 2007, *Cosmopolitanism*, London: Penguin.

Baudelaire, Charles, 1995 [1863], *The Painter of Modern Life and Other Essays*, ed. and trans. Jonathan Mayne, London: Phaidon.

Bauman, Zygmunt, 1993, *Postmodern Ethics*, London: Routledge.

Bell, David and Valentine, Gill, 1997, *Consuming Geographies: We are Where we Eat*, London: Routledge.

Blunt, Alison and Dowling, Robyn, 2007, *Home*, London: Routledge.

Bourdieu, Pierre, 1977, *Outline of a Theory of Practice*, trans. Richard Nice, Cambridge, MA: MIT Press.

Brendon, Piers, 1991, *Thomas Cook: 150 Years of Popular Tourism*, London: Secker and Warburg.

Bruce, Steve, 2011, *Secularization*, Oxford: Oxford University Press.

Bryman, Alan, 1995, *Disney and his Worlds*, London: Routledge.

Bryman, Alan, 1999, 'The Disneyization of Society', *Sociological Review* 47, pp. 25–47.

Bryson, Bill, 1999, *Notes from a Small Island*, London: BCA.

Buber, Martin, 2002 [1908], *The Legend of the Baal Shem*, trans. Maurice Friedman, London: Routledge.

Bunkse, Edmunds, 2004, *Geography and the Art of Life*, Baltimore, MD: Johns Hopkins University Press.

Butala, Sharon, 1991, *Upstream*, Toronto: Harper Collins.

Butala, Sharon, 1999 [1984], *Country of the Heart*, Toronto: Harper Collins.

Buzard, James, 1993, *The Beaten Track: European Tourism, Literature, and the Ways to Culture 1800–1918*, Oxford: Clarendon Press.

Buzard, James, 2002, 'The Grand Tour and after (1660–1840)', in Peter Hulme and Tim Youngs (eds), *The Cambridge Companion to Travel Writing*, Cambridge: Cambridge University Press, pp. 37–52.

Carter, Mike, 2012, *One Man and his Bike: A Life-changing Journey all the Way around the Coast of Britain*, London: Random House.

Chatwin, Bruce, 1987, *The Songlines*, London: Jonathan Cape.

Chesterton, Gilbert Keith, 2007 [1909], 'The Riddle of the Ivy', in G. K. Chesterton, *Tremendous Trifles*, New York: Cosimo Classics, pp. 92–4.

Clifford, James, 1997, *Routes: Travel and Translation in the Late Twentieth Century*, Cambridge, MA: Harvard University Press.

Codell, Julie F., 2007, 'Reversing the Grand Tour: Guest Discourse in Indian Travel Narratives', *Huntington Library Quarterly* 70, pp. 173–89.

Coelho, Pablo, 2006 [1988], *The Alchemist*, San Francisco: Harper Collins.

Coleman, Simon and Collins, Peter, 2006, 'The Shape of Faith or the Architectural Forms of the Religious Life', in Elisabeth Arweck and William Keenan (eds), *Materializing Religion*, Aldershot: Ashgate, pp. 32–44.

Coles, Anne and Walsh, Katie, 2010, 'From "Trucial State" to "Postcolonial" City? The Imaginative Geographies of British Expatriates in Dubai', *Journal of Ethnic and Migration Studies* 36, pp. 1317–33.

Crawford, Matthew, 2009, *The Case for Working with Your Hands: Or Why Office Work is Bad for Us and Fixing Things Feels Good*, Harmondsworth: Penguin.

Crompton, Peter, n.d., *Poem from a Train (Pathetic Am I)*, Wigan Railway Station.

Dant, T., 2004, 'The Driver-Car', *Theory, Culture and Society* 21, pp. 61–80.

de Botton, Alain, 2002, *The Art of Travel*, Harmondsworth: Penguin.

de Certeau, Michel, 1984, *The Practice of Everyday Life*, trans. Steven Rendell, Berkeley, CA: University of California Press.

de Certeau, Michel, 1992, *The Mystic Fable. Volume One: The Sixteenth and Seventeenth Centuries*, trans. Michael B. Smith, Chicago, IL: University of Chicago Press.

de Saint-Exupery, Antoine, 1996 [1945], *The Little Prince*, trans. Katherine Woods, London: Mammoth.

Dubisch, Jill, 2004, 'Heartland of America: Memory, Motion and the (Re)construction of History on a Motorcycle Pilgrimage', in Simon Coleman and John Eade (eds), *Reframing Pilgrimage: Cultures in Motion*, London: Routledge, pp. 105–32.

Dunbar, Robin I. M., 1992, 'Neocortex Size as a Constraint on Group Size in Primates', *Journal of Human Evolution* 22, pp. 469–93.

Evans, Katherine and Cheevers, Sarah, 1663, *A true account of the great tryals and cruel sufferings undergone by those two faithful servants of God, Katherine Evans and Sarah Cheevers . . . to which is added a short relation from George Robinson, of the sufferings which befel him in his journey to Jerusalem; and how God saved him from the hands of cruelty, when the sentence of death was passed against him*, London: R. Wilson.

Fenn, Richard. K., 1995, *The Persistence of Purgatory*, Cambridge: Cambridge University Press.

Fielding, Thomas, 1824, *Select Proverbs of All Nations*, London: John Wade.

Fortier, Anne-Marie, 2003, 'Making Home: Queer Migrations and Motions of Attachment', in Ahmed, S., Castaneda, C., Fortier, A.-M. and Sheller, M. (eds), *Uprootings/Regroundings: Questions of Home and Migration*, Oxford: Berg, pp. 115–35.

Friedberg, Anne, 1993, *Window Shopping: Cinema and the Postmodern*, Berkeley, CA: University of California Press.

Fuller, Patrick E., Lu, Jun and Saper, Clifford B., 2008, 'Differential Rescue of Light- and Food-Entrainable Circadian Rhythms', *Science* 320, pp. 1074–7.

Galgut, Damien, 2010, *In a Strange Room: Three Journeys*, London: Atlantic Books.

Gill, Dominic, 2010, *Take a Seat: One Man, One Tandem and Twenty Thousand Miles of Possibilities*, Edinburgh and London: Mainstream.

Goffman, Erving, 1963, *The Presentation of Self in Everyday Life*, London: Penguin.

Grahame, Kenneth, 1989 [1908], *The Wind in the Willows*, London: Methuen.

Grimshaw, Mike, 2008, *Bibles and Baedekers: Tourism, Travel, Exile and God*, London: Equinox.

REFERENCES

Hafiz, 2003, *The Subject Tonight Is Love: 60 Wild and Sweet Poems of Hafiz*, trans. Daniel Ladinsky, Harmondsworth: Penguin Compass.

Hahn, Scott, 2003, *The Lamb's Supper: The Mass as Heaven on Earth*, London: Darton, Longman and Todd.

Hanh, Thich Nhat, 1997, *The Long Road Turns to Joy: A Guide to Walking Meditation*, New Delhi: Full Circle.

Hebdige, Dick, 1979, *Subculture: The Meaning of Style*, London: Routledge.

Heelas, Paul and Woodhead, Linda with Benjamin Seel, Bronislaw Szerszynski and Karin Tusting, 2005, *The Spiritual Revolution: Why Religion is Giving Way to Spirituality*, Oxford: Blackwell.

Hibell, Ian, 1984, *Into the Remote Places*, London: Robson Books.

Hinds, Hilary, 2011, *George Fox and Early Quaker Culture*, Manchester: Manchester University Press.

Holland, Patrick and Huggan, Graham, 1998, *Tourists with Typewriters: Critical Reflections on Contemporary Travel Writing*, Ann Arbor, MI: University of Michigan Press.

Hughes, Gerard W., 1986, *In Search of a Way: Two Journeys of Spiritual Discovery*, London: Darton, Longman and Todd.

Hughes, Gerard W., 1991, *Walk to Jerusalem: In Search of Peace*, London: Darton, Longman and Todd.

Hurst, Charles E. and McConnell, David L., 2010, *An Amish Paradox: Diversity and Change in the World's Largest Amish Community*, Baltimore, MD: Johns Hopkins University Press.

It's a Wonderful Life, 1946, directed by Frank Capra, Liberty Films.

Iyengar, Sheena, 2010, *The Art of Choosing*, New York: Twelve.

Jakle, J., 1985, *The Tourist*, Lincoln: University of Nebraska Press.

Jones, Tobias, 2007, *Utopian Dreams*, London: Faber and Faber.

Joyce, Rachel, 2012, *The Unlikely Pilgrimage of Harold Fry*, London: Doubleday.

Kaplan, Caren, 1996, *Questions of Travel: Postmodern Discourses of Displacement*, Durham, NC: Duke University Press.

Kay, Jane Holtz, 1998, *Asphalt Nation: How the Automobile Took Over America and How We Can Take it Back*, Berkeley, CA: University of California Press.

Kerouac, Jack, 1972 [1955], *On the Road*, Harmondsworth: Penguin.

Kershner, Jon R., 2011, 'The (Com)Motion of Love: Theological Formation in John Woolman's Itinerant Ministry', *Quaker Religious Thought* 116–17, pp. 23–36.

Kershner, Jon. R., 2012, '"A more lively feeling": The correspondence and integration of mystical and spatial dynamics in John Woolman's travels', paper delivered at Borders and Crossings International Conference on Travel Writing, Woodbrooke Quaker Study Centre, Birmingham, England.

Knox, John, 2009, 'Sacro-egoism and the shifting paradigm of religiosity', unpublished PhD dissertation, University of Birmingham.

Kumar, Satish, 2008, 'Where Faith and Practice Meet', presentation to the Friends Association of Higher Education, Woodbrooke Quaker Study Centre, Birmingham, England.

le Guin, Ursula K., 1969, *The Left Hand of Darkness*, New York: Ace Publishing.

Leed, Eric J., 1991, *The Mind of the Traveller: From Gilgamesh to Global Tourism*, New York: Basic Books.

Lodge, David, 1984, *Small World: An Academic Romance*, London: Penguin.

Lodge, David, 1989, *Nice Work*, London: Penguin.

Lodge, David, 1991, *Paradise News*, London. Penguin.

McCall-Smith, Alexander, 2010, *The Double Comfort Safari Club*, London: Abacus.

Massey, Doreen, 2005, *For Space*, London: Sage.

Miller, Daniel, 2010, *Stuff*, Cambridge: Polity.

Morris, Meaghan, 1988, 'At Henry Parkes Motel', *Cultural Studies 2*, pp. 1–47.

Motion, Andrew, 2012, *Ramblings*, 17 March, BBC Radio 4.

Moulton, Philips P. (ed.), 1971, *The Journal and Major Essays of John Woolman*, Oxford: Oxford University Press.

Murphy, Dervla, 1965, *Full Tilt: Ireland to India with a Bicycle*, London: John Murray.

Night Mail, 1936, directed by Basil Wright and Harry Watt, GPO Film Unit.

Paterson, Matthew, 2007, *Automobile Politics: Ecology and Cultural Political Economy*, Cambridge: Cambridge University Press.

Phillips, Brian, 'Apocalypse without tears', in Pink Dandelion, Douglas Gwyn, Rachel Muers, Brian Phillips and Richard E. Sturm (eds), *Towards Tragedy/Reclaiming Hope: Literature, Theology and Sociology in Conversation*, Aldershot: Ashgate, 2004, pp. 57–76.

Phillips, Richard, 1997, *Mapping Men and Empire: A Geography of Adventure*, London: Routledge.

Pratt, Mary Louise, 1992, *Travel Writing and Transculturation*, London: Routledge.

Quaker Faith and Practice: The Book of Christian Discipline, 1995, London: Britain Yearly Meeting of the Religious Society of Friends (Quakers).

Ritzer, George, 1993, *The McDonaldization of Society*, Thousand Oaks, CA: Pine Forge Press.

Rohr, Richard, 2003, *Everything Belongs: The Gift of Contemplative Prayer*, New York: Crossroads.

Rohr, Richard, 2005, *Letting Go: A Spirituality of Subtraction*, audiobook, Cincinnati, OH: Franciscan Media.

Ruskin, John, 2002 [1865], *Sesame and Lilies*, ed. and Introduction by Deborah Epstein Nord, New Haven, CT: Yale University Press.

Sackville-West, Vita, 2007 [1926], *Passenger to Teheran*, London: I. B. Tauris.

Schivelbusch, Wolfgang, 1986, *The Railway Journey: The Industrialization and Perception of Time and Space in the 19th Century*, Berkeley, CA: University of California Press.

Sennett, Richard, 1977, *The Fall of Public Man*, New York: Knopf.

Setright, L. J. K., 2004, *Drive On! The Social History of the Motor Car*, London: Granta.

Shields, Rob, 1991, *Places on the Margin: Alternative Geographies of Modernity*, London: Routledge.

Sichel, Nina, 2004, 'Going Home', in Faith Eidse and Nina Sichel (eds), *Unrooted Childhoods: Memoirs of Growing up Global*, London: Nicholas Brealey Publishing, pp. 185–8.

Smith, Nigel, 1998, *The Journal of George Fox*, Harmondsworth: Penguin.

Solnit, Rebecca, 2002, *Wanderlust: A History of Walking*, London: Verso.

Somerville, C. John, 1992, *The Secularisation of Early Modern England: From Religious Culture to Religious Faith*, London: Oxford University Press.

Sontag, Susan, 1979, *On Photography*, Harmondsworth: Penguin.

Stevens, Sylvia, 2013, 'Travelling Ministry', in Stephen W. Angell and Pink Dandelion (eds), *The Oxford Handbook of Quaker Studies*, Oxford: Oxford University Press, pp. 292–305.

Stevenson, Robert Louis, 1881, *Virginibus Puerisque and Other Papers*, London: C. K. Paul.

Stevenson, Robert Louis, 1909 [1879], *Travels with a Donkey in the Cevennes*, London: Chatto and Windus.

Stockton, Shreve, 2008, *The Daily Coyote: A Story of Love, Survival and Trust in the Wilds of Wyoming*, New York: Simon and Schuster.

Suits, Bernard, 2005 [1978], *The Grasshopper: Games, Life and Utopia*, Broadview Press.

Swinglehurst, Edmund, 1983, *Thomas Cook*, London: Wayland.

The Truman Show, 1998, directed by Peter Weir, Paramount Pictures.

Thoreau, Henry David, 1995 [1854], *Walden: Or Life in the Woods*, New York: Dover.

Tolstoy, Leo, 1994 [1896], 'Civil Disobedience and Nonviolence' [drawn from 'Patriotism'], in Charles Chatfield and Ruzanna Ilukhina (eds), *Peace/Mir: An Anthology of Historic Alternatives to War*, New York: Syracuse University Press, p. 132.

Trades Union Congress, 2012, www.tuc.org.uk/workplace/tuc-21641-fo.cfm

Turner, Victor, 1974, *Dramas, Fields and Metaphors*, Ithaca, NY: Cornell University Press.

Twain, Mark, 2008 [1869], *The Innocents Abroad, or the new Pilgrims' Progress*, www.velvetelementbooks.com: Velvet Element Books.

Tweed, Thomas A., 2006, *Crossing and Dwelling: A Theory of Religion*, Cambridge, MA: Harvard University Press.

Up in the Air, 2009, directed by Jason Reitman, Paramount Pictures.

Urry, John, 1995, *Consuming Places*, London: Routledge.

Urry, John, 2002, *The Tourist Gaze*, 2nd edn, London: Sage 2002.

Urry, John, 2011, *Mobilities*, Cambridge: Polity.

Walker, Ian, 2007, 'Drivers overtaking bicyclists: objective data on the effects of riding position, helmet use, vehicle type and apparent gender', *Accident Analysis and Prevention* 39, pp. 417–25.

Waters, Nancy, 2010, 'Downward Travel', *Apartamento* 6, p. 16.

Waugh, Evelyn, 1947, *Decline and Fall*, London: Chapman and Hall.

Whitson, R. E., 1983, *The Shakers: Two Centuries of Spiritual Reflection*, New York: Paulist Press.

Wilde, Oscar, 2003 [1895], *The Importance of Being Earnest and Four Other Plays*, Introduction and Notes by Kenneth Krauss, New York: Fine Creative Media and Barnes and Noble.

REFERENCES

Wilson, Bryan R., 1982, *Religion in Sociological Perspective*, Oxford: Oxford University Press.

Winchester, Angus, 1993, 'The Discovery of the 1652 Country', *Friends Quarterly* October, pp. 373–83.

Wolf, Daniel, 1991, *The Rebels: A Brotherhood of Outlaw Bikers*, Toronto: University of Toronto Press.

Woolf, Virginia, 1938, *Three Guineas*, New York: Harcourt Brace Jovanovich.

Woolman, John, 1922 [1758], Serious Considerations on Trade', in Amelia M. Gummere, *The Journal and Essays of John Woolman*, London: Macmillan, pp. 397–400.

Woolman, John, 1925, 'John Woolman to Rachel Wilson, July 30, 1772', *Journal of the Friends' Historical Society* 22, p. 18.